CW00499053

# In the Beginning

# In the Beginning

## *Bible readings for the first weeks of parenting*

Stephen and Jacqui Hance

Text copyright © Stephen and Jacqui Hance 2000

The authors assert the moral right
to be identified as the authors of this work

Published by
**The Bible Reading Fellowship**
Peter's Way, Sandy Lane West
Oxford OX4 5HG
ISBN 1 84101 078 2

First published 2000
10 9 8 7 6 5 4 3 2 1 0

All rights reserved

**Acknowledgments**
Scripture quotations taken from The New Revised Standard Version of the Bible, Anglicized Edition, copyright © 1989, 1995 by the Division of Christian Education of the National Council of the Churches of Christ in the USA, are used by permission. All rights reserved.

Scripture quotations taken from the *Holy Bible, New International Version*, copyright © 1973, 1978, 1984 by International Bible Society, are used by permission of Hodder & Stoughton Limited. All rights reserved. 'NIV' is a registered trademark of International Bible Society. UK trademark number 1448790.

A catalogue record for this book is available from the British Library

Printed and bound in Great Britain by
Caledonian International Book Manufacturing Ltd, Glasgow

# Foreword

Two weeks ago our eldest son graduated from university. There was—as they say—hardly a dry eye in the house. It was a special moment.

Later, we recalled another special moment nearly twenty-two years ago, in a side room of a maternity unit when we studied him as a newborn, red and wrinkled miracle.

Much water has flowed under the bridge between those two landmark events. Lots of laughter and quite a few tears. Some anxious moments and many happy ones. Times when we believed we were the worst parents in the universe and others when we basked in the glow of our son's achievements. There were times when we wanted to hug him to death and others when we... um, well... felt less loving.

Being a parent is a lifetime spent on an emotional rollercoaster—and one of the greatest privileges in the world.

Stephen and Jacqui Hance have written a book we'd love to have received as a gift as we set out as new parents. It is full of encouragement and wise insights. The Bible readings, comments and prayers lift the lid on what God thinks about the joy and privilege of bringing up children. It's a book that reminds us that parenting is a calling, not a job, and points us beyond our own resources to the grace of God.

Mums and dads (especially new ones) need all the help they can get—and here is a book that sets them off on the right track.

*Ian and Ruth Coffey*

# Contents

## NEW RESOURCES



## NEW LIFESTYLE



## NEW LOVE

# Introduction

The decision to have a baby is one of the most life-changing choices any of us will make. More demanding than getting married, more irrevocable than a career change, few of us quite appreciate what it will really be like until we have done it. By any measure, having a baby is one of the most stressful experiences that we can have.

That doesn't mean that it is not a good and exciting experience. For most people, it is. We experience feelings of joy and love and delight in the first weeks of parenthood that may be unlike anything we have felt before. But we also go through enormous change. Our sense of who we are and what is important to us may change dramatically. Our relationships with spouse, parents and other children may change. For some parents, there will be changes in employment, and most will find that their social life undergoes change as well. The extent of involvement in church may well change, and there will probably be change in our relationship with God and our spiritual life too.

That is where this book comes in. As parents of three children ourselves, we have been through all these changes and more. We know what it is like to try to work out a new pattern to life as a growing family, and to do it in the light of scripture. The problem is that any kind of regular Bible reading and prayer can easily go straight out of the window when life seems to consist of broken nights and endless dirty nappies. This book is designed to help.

Each chapter consists of a reading from the Bible, followed by some thoughts and reflections which relate the passage to our situation as parents, and finally a short prayer.

The chapters are grouped in sections with overall headings, generally consisting of six chapters apiece, although one is shorter and one is longer. This is simply because the readings we chose seemed to fit into subject groups in this way. There are forty-two chapters in all, so if you read one every day it will take you six weeks to finish the book. But you don't have to read one every day. If you only read three or four per week, that is fine. Please don't feel that if you miss a day you are getting behind and need to catch up. You don't! Take your time, and read at your own pace. There is enough to do as a new parent without feeling guilty because you can't keep up with a routine of daily prayer and Bible reading.

We have deliberately given everything—reading, notes and prayer—in full, to make this book as easy to use as possible. Any time you get five or ten minutes free, you can use it. It may be while feeding, or sitting in the park halfway through a stroll, or on the bus to work. It is intended to be read by mother or father, or by both together. Perhaps both parents might read it separately and then discuss it together. It is up to you. It can be read after the birth of a first child or subsequent children, or after adopting a baby or child. It can be read during the very first days and weeks of a baby's life, or some time later on.

Many of us find that our picture of God changes when we become parents. On the one hand, we may have seen ourselves as serving God, pleasing him by the amount of time we spend in prayer or attending church activities. Now most of that may have to stop. Perhaps for the first time, we have to learn that it is God who holds on to us by his grace, not we who hold on to him by our hard work. On the other hand, as we are overwhelmed by love and joy as we look at our new baby, so we sense something of what

God experiences us when he looks at us, his children. We sense his commitment to us, his acceptance of us, his delight in us.

Our prayer is that this will be your experience, and that this book will help you both to adjust to the thrills and spills of parenthood, and to understand more of God's parental love for you.

*Stephen and Jacqui Hance*

# Thank God!

**Psalm 148 (NRSV)**

Praise the Lord!
Praise the Lord from the heavens;
praise him in the heights!
Praise him, all his angels;
praise him, all his host!
Praise him, sun and moon;
praise him, all you shining stars!
Praise him, you highest heavens,
and you waters above the heavens!
Let them praise the name of the Lord,
for he commanded and they were created.
He established them forever and ever;
he fixed their bounds, which cannot be passed.
Praise the Lord from the earth,
you sea monsters and all deeps,
fire and hail, snow and frost,
stormy wind fulfilling his command!
Mountains and all hills,
fruit trees and all cedars!
Wild animals and all cattle,
creeping things and flying birds!
Kings of the earth and all peoples,
princes and all rulers of the earth!
Young men and women alike,
old and young together!
Let them praise the name of the Lord,
for his name alone is exalted;
his glory is above earth and heaven.
He has raised up a horn for his people,
praise for all his faithful,
for the people of Israel who are close to him.
Praise the Lord!

At 12.17 a.m. on 17 February 1999, I became a father for the third time. I watched helpless, awestruck, as powerful forces too primal for mere words overtook Jacqui's body, and turned her from creature to creator. As the midwives and I tried to present ourselves as a team, ready to support and willing to bear the brunt of Jacqui's pain, we all knew that in reality this was no team effort. Only Jacqui was truly experiencing the rapture and horror of giving birth. My endlessly rehearsed encouragements to 'breathe through it' seemed weak and thin by comparison with the drama taking place before my eyes. When at last it was over, the waves of joy and relief were almost overwhelming. Weeks later, the incredible fact that here is a new little person who was not here before, and who will be part of our lives for ever, still hasn't sunk in. Perhaps it never completely does.

Mythology is full of stories of magicians and kings who sought the power to turn base metal into gold. What a waste of time. When you have watched a woman give birth, alchemy seems trivial by comparison. It occurred to me while I was in the delivery room of that hospital that if men are driven by a desire to rule the world, it is probably derived from a psychological need to over-compensate for the fact that only women can produce the miracle of life.

Since you are reading this book, you have probably been through a similar experience recently, as birth-giver or onlooker. Of course, our experiences aren't identical. A midwife who had attended many deliveries said to us, 'Every labour is different.' You may recently have experienced the birth of your first child, or your fourth. The labour may have been long and frustrating, or quick and exhilarating. Your joy at the birth of your child may have been tempered by other emotions, perhaps anxiety about how you are going to provide for a child whom you had not planned to have, or heartache over a child born in need of some special care and attention. Or it may be that you were not present when your child was born, perhaps because someone else was the biological parent, and this gift came to you by some other means.

Whatever the circumstances for you and your child, most of us find birth an awe-inspiring experience. Even atheists and agnostics can find themselves touched by a sense of the wonder of it all. Many feel the need to pray, or to acknowledge God perhaps for the first time—hence the continuing demand for baptism and thanksgiving services even from non-churchgoers. We hear ourselves saying 'Thank God!'—and meaning it—when our child is safely brought into the world.

Psalm 148 helps us to give expression to that sense of thankfulness. It is a wonderful song of worship, a series of exhortations to offer praise to the Creator of all that is. Little is said about why God is worthy of such praise. This is not one of those psalms which lists the past great interventions of the Lord in the life of his people. The main reasons we are given for worship are that God has created all things by his word (v. 5) and that his glory is seen in what he has created (v. 13).

In the first half of the psalm (vv. 1–6), the heavens are called upon to praise God. We are presented with a wonderful picture of the cosmos united in praise. Sun, moon and stars, and the heavenly host, are to worship the Lord. In the second section (vv. 7–14), the earth is exhorted to respond. It is not only people—not even mainly people—who are to praise God, but every created thing. The inhabitants of the mysterious deep, the frightening elements, the plants and animals and human beings of every age and status are to join in this symphony of praise. This praise surely cannot be merely words spoken and sung. Only sentient beings can worship God in that way. This is the praise that arises when the wonderful creatures of God simply are as God intended them to be. This is the glory of the Lord reflected back to him by the beauty of his creation.

Various religious groups—some of them ostensibly Christian—have believed that the material world is at best morally neutral, at worst totally corrupt. According to this view, spiritual growth comes when we manage to detach ourselves from the world around us, and focus on other more holy things. The world is a distraction from God. In contrast, the Bible teaches that God is revealed, in part, in the wonder of what he has created. We see his glory in the beauty of glorious countryside, in the power of angry seas, in the bustle of the city. We see his glory in each other. And I can't stop thinking about how I see his glory in the birth of my new child, and in the ceaseless growth and change of my other children.

Why doesn't the psalmist spell this out? Because words cannot do justice to it. If you have seen God's glory in a sunset, a community, a birth, you can't fully give expression to what you have seen. All you can do is bow before the One whose wonder is revealed before you and give him worship. Use Psalm 148 to help you join with the rest of creation in worshipping him today.

**Prayer**

*Dear Creator God, we worship and praise you for the wonder of the universe you have made. We especially thank you for the miracle of the new child you have entrusted to us. Help us never to lose the sense of awe at your great goodness and power. Help us never to cease to worship you for your gifts to us. Amen*

# In the beginning

**Genesis 1:1–3, 6, 9, 11, 14, 20–23 (NRSV)**

In the beginning when God created the heavens and the earth, the earth was a formless void and darkness covered the face of the deep, while a wind from God swept over the face of the waters. Then God said, 'Let there be light'; and there was light...

And God said, 'Let there be a dome in the midst of the waters, and let it separate the waters from the waters.'...

And God said, 'Let the waters under the sky be gathered together into one place, and let the dry land appear.' And it was so...

Then God said, 'Let the earth put forth vegetation: plants yielding seed, and fruit trees of every kind on earth that bear fruit with the seed in it.' And it was so...

And God said, 'Let there be lights in the dome of the sky to separate the day from the night; and let them be for signs and for seasons and for days and years.'...

And God said, 'Let the waters bring forth swarms of living creatures, and let birds fly above the earth across the dome of the sky.' So God created the great sea monsters and every living creature that moves, of every kind, with which the waters swarm, and every winged bird of every kind. And God saw that it was good. God blessed them, saying, 'Be fruitful and multiply and fill the waters in the seas, and let birds multiply on the earth.'

And there was evening and there was morning, the fifth day.

In the previous reading, we were encouraged to praise God for the wonder of his creation. We also noted how, in childbirth, we become creators too. We share with God in his creative work.

Over the next four readings, we are going to look at the story of how God created the world, and how this good creation was marred by human foolishness and disobedience, from the first four chapters of Genesis. Two of the readings we will be using—including today's—are too long to be reproduced here in their entirety, but we would encourage you to read the whole passage from the Bible. This would be a good moment to pause and read Genesis 1:1–23 if you have time.

The first chapters of Genesis all too easily become a theological football. One side argues that they are historically accurate, and the other insists that science has shown them to be 'untrue'. We have no desire to step into that controversy. However, it seems clear to us that whatever position we take in this debate, there is a lot to be gained from this story. Genesis 1—4 tells us about where we come from, about the God who created us and his purposes in creating us. It tells us what our attitude to the rest of creation should be. It helps us to account for both the beauty we see in the world around us and the darkness in the world of which we are aware. The story of the creation and the fall gives a realistic picture. It teaches us about the goodness of creation, and the flawed nature of it—and of us. It rings true both with the teaching of the Bible that God is good and powerful, and with our own experience of a world gone wrong.

In the beginning, God created. There was nothing, but out of that nothing God brought forth a cosmos of infinite beauty and variety. He called into being the most dazzling star, the deepest black hole, the most delicate flower, the tiniest grub. In the wild joy of his extravagant creation, he designed more species of insects than anyone is going to be able to count, whole solar systems that nobody will ever see, creatures which, try as we might, we can't see any purpose for. In the history of human creativity nobody has ever been able to create anything that comes close to the splendour of the world God made.

We were visiting the Uffizi gallery in Florence one summer evening. Around some of the most striking or famous works of art on display, small groups of visitors gathered, talking, taking photos and listening to their audio guides. At one end of a long corridor we saw a group far larger than any other, captivated by whatever it was they were looking at. What could it be? As we got closer, we saw the object of their fascination. They were staring not at a painting or a sculpture, but out of the window. Outside it was nightfall. The sun was going down behind the city, and the sight was spectacular. Nothing else on display in that gallery could rival the beauty of that sunset. Even the pinnacle of human creativity was but a pale reflection of God's work.

When an artist is working on a piece, he may invest months, even years of his life into it. He may keep coming back to it, changing it, improving it, until the earlier work is entirely obscured by the later. But the time must come when he decides the work is finished, that he is satisfied with it. At some stage he must stop work, step back, and decide that what he has made is good.

When God had created the universe, he took a step back, and declared that his work was good. As he completed each section of his work of art, he was satisfied with it. Each part inspired him to still greater triumphs until the masterpiece was complete. Each step built upon what had been done before. There was a purpose to the sequence of events, an order to it. Animals had to be created after vegetation. Vegetation had to be created after the dry land. Any other order would not have worked. God took the chaos that existed before the universe was made, and imposed order upon it.

Pregnancy and childbirth work in the same way. There is an order to them. They work because things happen in the right sequence. They are purposeful, not chaotic, however much it may feel at times as if the reverse is true. The woman giving birth does not have to decide in what sequence things will happen. They happen naturally. This is how she is designed.

No painter or sculptor who gazed with satisfaction upon a completed work of art ever did so with as much joy as the parent picking up a newly born baby in the delivery room. We look at this masterpiece, this tiny human being, with wonder. 'Look at his little fingers!' we exclaim. 'Listen to her cry!' At that moment we share in God's pleasure as he looked at all that he had made. 'It is good,' he says, and we are forced to agree.

**Prayer**

*Father God, you looked with joy at all you had made and declared it good. We look at the child you have made through us, and share your joy. Please help us to go on shaping and making this child into the person you want them to be, so that you and we may continue to rejoice in them. Amen*

# The pinnacle of creation

**Genesis 1:26—2:3 (NRSV)**

Then God said, 'Let us make humankind in our image, according to our likeness; and let them have dominion over the fish of the sea, and over the birds of the air, and over the cattle, and over all the wild animals of the earth, and over every creeping thing that creeps upon the earth.'

So God created humankind in his image, in the image of God he created them; male and female he created them.

God blessed them, and God said to them, 'Be fruitful and multiply, and fill the earth and subdue it; and have dominion over the fish of the sea and over the birds of the air and over every living thing that moves upon the earth.' God said, 'See, I have given you every plant yielding seed that is upon the face of all the earth, and every tree with seed in its fruit; you shall have them for food. And to every beast of the earth, and to every bird of the air, and to everything that creeps on the earth, everything that has the breath of life, I have given every green plant for food.' And it was so. God saw everything that he had made, and indeed, it was very good. And there was evening and there was morning, the sixth day.

Thus the heavens and the earth were finished, and all their multitude. And on the seventh day God finished the work that he had done, and he rested on the seventh day from all the work that he had done. So God blessed the seventh day and hallowed it, because on it God rested from all the work that he had done in creation.

In the previous reading, we read about how God created the universe, the world and the non-human creatures that populate it and, like an artist viewing his completed masterpiece with satisfaction, declared it good. Today in our reading we see the pinnacle of God's creation, the final piece of the jigsaw—the creation of humankind. Only after God has placed men and women in the centre of the picture does he declare it '*very* good' (1:31).

God expresses pleasure in everything he has made, but only people are said to be made in his image: 'Then God said, "Let us make humankind in our image, according to our likeness"' (1:26).

What does it mean to be made in the image or likeness of God? Theologians have spent gallons of ink on this vexed question. Some people have assumed that this refers to a physical likeness. As a result, God has often been portrayed in religious art looking like a man, usually an elderly gentleman in need of a shave and haircut. But this is not what the text means.

Many writers have picked up on attributes of God which humans also share to explain what it means to be made in God's image, for example self-awareness, a sense of what is morally right and wrong, the capacity for rational thought. Others have focused on the ability to make relationships, noting that God is Trinity ('Let *us* make humankind' hints at this), and that we human beings likewise reach our potential and find fulfilment only in relationship, with one another and with God.

Whilst there may be truth in many of these ideas, the context of the passage suggests that we should look at one aspect in particular. To be made in God's image is to have dominion over the rest of creation. In Genesis 1:26, the declaration of intent, 'Let us make humankind in our image', is immediately followed with 'Let them have dominion...' over the fish, the birds, the animals, and the creepy-crawlies.

This dominion isn't about reckless tyranny and selfish misuse of the created world, as some have interpreted it. It is to be modelled on God's own lordship, which is caring, nurturing and creative. In one sense, men and women are to be God's representatives on earth, sharing with him in his responsibility for the whole creation. To be completely human is to consciously and wholeheartedly represent God in this way—which is why Jesus was the most complete human being who has ever lived.

This is made specific in the New Testament, in the story Jesus told about a landowner and his tenant farmers (Matthew 21:33–41). Here the landowner is a picture of God, and the tenants represent the human race, whose responsibility it is to care for the land as the owner requires. We are not to read into this that God is an absentee landlord, uninterested in the world as long as people are doing their job satisfactorily. Rather, he invites us to share with him in his work of care and stewardship.

God also invites us to share with him in his work of creating, when he commands people to 'be fruitful and multiply' (1:28). It has been said that this is the only one of God's commands that the human race has had no difficulty in obeying! But there is far more to this than reproduction. It is part of our stewardship of the world that we should share in God's creativity. We see the evidence for this God-given creativity all around us, in art and science, in music and literature, in the ways in which people interact with one another and create community together. We should be able to see it in our families, in the ways in which we shape and influence each other.

God's command to exercise this kind of dominion, in nurture and creativity, is of particular relevance to us as new parents. The awesome work of giving birth is clearly a response to this command, but so is everything that comes after. No child is born fully created. We go on creating this new person in the love we give and the example we set for many years to come. To share in this creative work of God's is the most wonderful privilege.

It is also exhausting. God created and then he rested. In doing so he set a pattern for us to follow. That rest did not mark the end of his creative work, for he is still about it today. But it marked a break. We as parents will not reach the end of our work for a long time to come, but we too need to follow God's pattern of work and rest, and to encourage each other in it, if we are to be able to sustain our efforts.

**Prayer**

*Heavenly Father, we thank you that you have entrusted us with dominion over your creation. Give us wisdom as we exercise it, particularly in our new role as parents. May we do so with integrity, following your example, through Jesus Christ our Lord. Amen*

# Mixed blessings

**Genesis 3:1–8, 16–19 (NRSV)**

Now the serpent was more crafty than any other wild animal that the Lord God had made. He said to the woman, 'Did God say, "You shall not eat from any tree in the garden"?' The woman said to the serpent, 'We may eat of the fruit of the trees in the garden; but God said, "You shall not eat of the fruit of the tree that is in the middle of the garden, nor shall you touch it, or you shall die."' But the serpent said to the woman, 'You will not die; for God knows that when you eat of it your eyes will be opened, and you will be like God, knowing good and evil.' So when the woman saw that the tree was good for food, and that it was a delight to the eyes, and that the tree was to be desired to make one wise, she took of its fruit and ate; and she also gave some to her husband, who was with her, and he ate. Then the eyes of both were opened, and they knew that they were naked; and they sewed fig leaves together and made loincloths for themselves.

They heard the sound of the Lord God walking in the garden at the time of the evening breeze, and the man and his wife hid themselves from the presence of the Lord God among the trees of the garden…

To the woman God said, 'I will greatly increase your pangs in childbearing; in pain you shall bring forth children, yet your desire shall be for your husband, and he shall rule over you.' And to the man he said, 'Because you have listened to the voice of your wife, and have eaten of the tree about which I commanded you, "You shall not eat of it," cursed is the ground because of you; in toil you shall eat of it all the days of your life; thorns and thistles it shall bring forth for you; and you shall eat the plants of the field. By the sweat of your face you shall eat bread until you return to the ground, for out of it you were taken; you are dust, and to dust you shall return.'

We have again edited this passage from Genesis 3, but if you have the time you may find it helpful to read the whole passage, from verse 1 through to 19.

Some of us may find this a rather difficult passage to read at this stage. Firstly, there are the historical problems inevitably raised by stories including such creatures as talking serpents. Secondly, there are the moral problems raised by God's curse of the world and its inhabitants, particularly the woman's punishment of increased pain in childbirth—something you may have strong feelings about at the moment! Thirdly, we may feel that this passage brings us back to earth with too severe a bump when we may still be caught up in the euphoria which can follow the birth of a child.

However, there are strong reasons for looking at this passage now. The story of the fall of humankind is true both to our experience and to the teaching of the rest of the Bible.

First of all, it is true to our experience. The newborn baby lying asleep in his cot may strike an angelic figure, but he doesn't need to be very much older before we see signs of imperfection in him. In the next section, we will look more closely at this issue. But it is worth noting now that, just as God watched while the creation he had declared good slipped into rebellion against his will, so every parent to some degree has to acknowledge that the child they have created does not live up to aspirations either.

Secondly, it is true to the teaching of the Bible. The Bible routinely acknowledges, in both Old and New Testaments, that the human condition is characterized by sin and suffering, as well as goodness and blessing, the legacy both of God's good creation and the fall from grace that followed it. This story only makes the point in narrative form.

So even children are themselves shaped by both the creation and the fall. They are inheritors of both the image of God and the frailty of Adam and Eve. It may be difficult for us to acknowledge the truth of this with very young children, but as soon as they are old enough to give expression to what is in them, we see it all too clearly. The signs of this are there from the very beginning. In childbirth itself, the pain of labour is mixed with wonder at what is actually taking place. Immediately afterwards, the cry of the newborn baby may produce tears of joy, whilst in weeks to come, the same cry will produce tears of frustration. It isn't always easy to separate out what, in us or our experience, comes from God's good creation, and what comes from the corruption of that creation.

This is true for all children, but the ways in which it is true may vary from child to child. However, it is striking how, as our children grow, we see so many of the actions and attitudes that Adam and Eve exhibited displayed in them. In the story of the fall, we see active disobedience to clear instructions, attraction to something which has been forbidden, an eagerness to blame one another for what has gone wrong. None of these things is unknown to parents of even fairly young children.

When children begin to speak, the word they are generally encouraged to say is 'Mummy' or 'Daddy'. The word they are most likely to use with feeling is 'No'. People started saying 'No' at the fall, and our children pick up the habit when they are still small.

None of this is to argue against what we have been saying in the last few readings about the wonder of each new child. Every child is made in God's image, an awesome gift from our Creator to us. The right response to that gift is gratitude, joy, worship of the gift-giver. But if we only think about the goodness of it all, we will be unprepared for the reality of life in our world and in our families, where experience is always more mixed. We may also be unprepared for the shortcomings as parents which each of us will display in the years ahead. We need to begin our family life with awe and celebration but also with our eyes open, so that our expectations of our children, our partners and ourselves can be realistic; and we are reminded to keep coming back to God for his help.

**Prayer**

*Heavenly Father, as we look at the world and see how far removed it is from your perfect creation, we acknowledge our need of your help and guidance as we attempt to be good parents. Please give us grace and strength as we care and nurture, and help us to be realistic in our expectations of ourselves, our children and others. Amen*

# When something is wrong

**Genesis 4:1–16 (NRSV)**

Now the man knew his wife Eve, and she conceived and bore Cain, saying, 'I have produced a man with the help of the Lord.' Next she bore his brother Abel. Now Abel was a keeper of sheep, and Cain a tiller of the ground. In the course of time Cain brought to the Lord an offering of the fruit of the ground, and Abel for his part brought of the firstlings of his flock, their fat portions. And the Lord had regard for Abel and his offering, but for Cain and his offering he had no regard. So Cain was very angry, and his countenance fell. The Lord said to Cain, 'Why are you angry, and why has your countenance fallen? If you do well, will you not be accepted? And if you do not do well, sin is lurking at the door; its desire is for you, but you must master it.'

Cain said to his brother Abel, 'Let us go out to the field.' And when they were in the field, Cain rose up against his brother Abel, and killed him. Then the Lord said to Cain, 'Where is your brother Abel?' He said, 'I do not know; am I my brother's keeper?' And the Lord said, 'What have you done? Listen; your brother's blood is crying out to me from the ground! And now you are cursed from the ground, which has opened its mouth to receive your brother's blood from your hand. When you till the ground, it will no longer yield to you its strength; you will be a fugitive and a wanderer on the earth.' Cain said to the Lord, 'My punishment is greater than I can bear! Today you have driven me away from the soil, and I shall be hidden from your face; I shall be a fugitive and a wanderer on the earth, and anyone who meets me may kill me.' Then the Lord said to him, 'Not so! Whoever kills Cain will suffer a sevenfold vengeance.' And the Lord put a mark on Cain, so that no one who came upon him would kill him. Then Cain went away from the presence of the Lord, and settled in the land of Nod, east of Eden.

Today we received a prayer letter from some missionary friends who are working in an African country. They reported that their one-year-old daughter had spent a frightening time in hospital recently, suffering from high temperatures and convulsions. The letter spoke of the heartache of seeing their little girl so ill without knowing what was wrong, and the joy of the recovery that has now taken place.

None of us are parents for very long without experiencing heartache along with the joy. In verse 1 of our reading for today, we read of Eve's joy in the birth of her first child. 'I have produced a man with the help of the Lord,' Eve declared, naming her child Cain, which sounds like the Hebrew for 'produced'. But only seven verses later, the elder son has turned on the younger, and Eve has lost them both.

Eve's son grew up angry and bitter. The first family was the first dysfunctional family. We may wonder what had gone wrong in the years that the Bible account skips over. Did Cain always have a violent temper? Was the sibling relationship always sparking with the potential for danger? Did the parents treat the younger more gently, so stoking up resentment in the elder? Did Cain learn from the example of his parents that rules were not for keeping, that you could do what you wanted and ignore the consequences?

Whatever had transpired as Cain and Abel were growing up, the final confrontation between them tore their family apart. Alongside the pain of losing one son to death and another to exile, Adam and Eve must have known the disappointment that asks, 'How did our child turn out like this?' It's a question many parents have asked since.

Every parent experiences heartache and disappointment at some point. Whenever we love someone, we open ourselves to pain as well as joy, and with our children the love is more intimate and the vulnerability more complete than in almost any other relationship, so the pain can be more acute than in almost any other relationship.

It may be, as for Adam and Eve, the pain of watching a child grow up to be rebellious or angry, distant from the rest of the family. It may be, as for Adam and Eve, the anguish of the loss of a child. It may be the far milder disappointment of realizing that our child is not as academic or socially outgoing or ambitious as we had hoped. It may be the dawning realization that something is not quite right with our child, that they have some defect or illness which is going to colour their lives in some way.

As we have had children, and our friends have had children, it has been something of a shock to discover how many are born with something wrong. Most of these problems will make only a marginal difference to the child's life. Many would have gone unnoticed only a few years ago, and require little or no treatment. Even with these, there may be a sense of disappointment and worry. For a small number of children, the realization comes during pregnancy or shortly after birth that something is wrong which is going to affect the whole course of that child's life.

Jacqui used to work with adults with severe learning difficulties; it was a very challenging and rewarding job. She was constantly amazed and impressed by some of the families with which she had contact. Throughout each person's life there had been heartache and tears. Sometimes it had taken years for the parents to come to terms with their situation, but in case after case there were also times of real happiness. As expectations and aspirations adjusted to reality, then joy appeared in unimaginable places. One lady who had Downs Syndrome had been unable to speak, but around the time of her twenty-first birthday she said her first word: 'lager'! Her mother was so proud! All parents will have to re-evaluate their plans for their children at times. The parents of a child with any type of congenital defect will need to adjust their future plans accordingly, but the future will hold many joys as well as the frustrations and disappointments of parenting.

At the end of today's reading, God promises Cain that even though he is going to become a restless wanderer, God's seal of protection will be upon him. As our children grow and we experience times of anxiety, we too can learn to trust God to protect and care for them.

Recently we accepted an invitation to move to a different church in a new area. Stephen was concerned about the effect that these changes might have on our children. One night he had a dream. In the dream our children were playing on a beach. Meanwhile, we parents were enjoying a ride at a fairground which overlooked the beach. At times the children were out of our sight, and we became more and more anxious about them, but we could not get off the ride until it had finished. When the ride was over, we ran to the beach, only to find the children playing happily in the sand. The next morning, as he thought about his dream, Stephen felt that God was saying that, even though we couldn't always watch over our children ourselves, God was taking care of them, and he would always continue to do so.

**Prayer**

*Heavenly Father, thank you that you watch over us and our children. Please give us grace and courage each day, so that we may cope with the struggles and heartache as well as the joys of parenting. May we always be aware of your hand in our family life. Amen*

# God's promise to us

**Revelation 21:1–7 (NSRV)**

Then I saw a new heaven and a new earth; for the first heaven and the first earth had passed away, and the sea was no more. And I saw the holy city, the new Jerusalem, coming down out of heaven from God, prepared as a bride adorned for her husband. And I heard a loud voice from the throne saying, 'See, the home of God is among mortals. He will dwell with them as their God; they will be his peoples, and God himself will be with them; he will wipe every tear from their eyes. Death will be no more; mourning and crying and pain will be no more, for the first things have passed away.'

And the one who was seated on the throne said, 'See, I am making all things new.' Also he said, 'Write this, for these words are trustworthy and true.' Then he said to me, 'It is done! I am the Alpha and the Omega, the beginning and the end. To the thirsty I will give water as a gift from the spring of the water of life. Those who conquer will inherit these things, and I will be their God and they will be my children.'

The Bible tells us many stories, but it also gives us one overarching story, to which each individual story relates in some way. Over the last four readings, we have been looking at the first part of this big story. Today we see how the story ends.

The big story begins with hope and promise, and then tragically goes wrong. God creates a beautiful world, and men and women who are like him in their creativity and their longing for relationship, and he gives them real responsibility for his wonderful creation. Almost straight away they forget why they have been created, and become self-absorbed and disobedient. The consequences are immense, for the first family and everyone who has come since.

The rest of the Bible can be read as an account of God's action to put right what went wrong in that first act of rebellion. In the history books of the Old Testament, we read how God sought to remind his people of his activity on their behalf. In the Law, God's people were called back to a lifestyle in keeping with his purposes for the world. In the prophets, we hear the voice of God the Father, sometimes angry, sometimes pleading, urging that his people should recall who he is and who they are, and return to right worship and right living. In the Gospels, we are confronted with the awesome love and self-sacrifice of God who comes to earth in the person of Jesus to bring women and men into his kingdom. In the letters of the New Testament, we are taught how those of us who have come into God's Church are to think and live.

Now we come to the end of the story. Looking into the future, John, the writer of Revelation, sees a time when God's purposes will at last be fulfilled, when the terrible legacy of human rejection of God will finally be destroyed. It is a time when God lives side-by-side with his people. It is a time when pain and suffering and death are at last conquered. It is a time when the last tears of God's people are gently wiped away by God himself.

This picture of the future is God's promise to us. In the previous reading, we looked at the issues which arise when something goes wrong with our child. Today's reading assures us that there will come a time when all that is less than perfect in the created order is put right. All sorrow will vanish, all anxieties will finally be laid to rest, as God's perfect will for us is at last put into full effect.

Why is this important? Why is it here in the Bible? Because when John received his vision and put it into words, the Church was suffering persecution. While some Christians were being martyred, others were defecting from the faith under the pressure. God revealed this vision of the future to John in part because he knew that when people are suffering, it helps to know that the pain won't last for ever. The Christians of John's day could take courage from the promise that a great and glorious future awaited them. Strengthened by this knowledge, they could hold on to their faith even through the struggles of their time.

Human nature hasn't changed since the time of Revelation. We still get through difficult times by looking to the future. A woman in childbirth knows her pain won't last for ever, and at the end she will have the child she has wanted. Her midwife might urge her to think about the baby on the way when the experience seems overwhelming, and the reminder that her present struggle will come to a joyful end can be enough to strengthen her for the task.

The same principle holds true in other areas of life. At the time of writing, our third child is one month old, and we are experiencing again the ingrained fatigue that sets in around this time. After a gap of four years since our second child was born, we had forgotten quite what it was like! But we do know from past experience that it doesn't last for ever. Every time we find ourselves falling asleep in front of the TV at nine o'clock in the evening, or failing to form coherent sentences in conversation, we remind ourselves that it's only a phase. This experience doesn't last for ever. It will pass.

There is a danger in thinking like this. We can become people who are always living for tomorrow, the kind of people who always say they will be happy just as soon as such-and-such a thing takes place. Of course, when it does take place, everything still isn't perfect, and so contentment is deferred until something else happens.

That attitude is not what we are commending. We need to learn to live for each day, to appreciate each moment for what it is, rather than decrying it for what it is not. But there are times when it all gets too much, and when it does it can help to reassure ourselves—and each other—that it will pass.

**Prayer**

*Dear Heavenly Father, thank you that a time is coming when all pain and heartache will end, when we will see you face to face, and you will wipe away every tear. Please help us now to live for each moment, but also, when things become too much, to draw hope and courage from the future. Amen*

# Co-creators with God

**Psalm 139:7–16 (NIV)**

Where can I go from your Spirit?
  Where can I flee from your presence?
If I go up to the heavens, you are there;
  if I make my bed in the depths, you are there.
If I rise on the wings of the dawn,
  if I settle on the far side of the sea,
even there your hand will guide me,
  your right hand will hold me fast.
If I say, 'Surely the darkness will hide me
  and the light become night around me,'
even the darkness will not be dark to you;
  the night will shine like the day,
  for darkness is as light to you.
For you created my inmost being;
  you knit me together in my mother's womb.
I praise you because I am fearfully and wonderfully made;
  your works are wonderful,
  I know that full well.
My frame was not hidden from you
  when I was made in the secret place.
When I was woven together in the depths of the earth,
  your eyes saw my unformed body.
All the days ordained for me
  were written in your book
  before one of them came to be.

We were leaving an antenatal class during Jacqui's first pregnancy. We had been finding out about the incredible journey that the baby makes from its mother's womb to the outside world, and how the woman's body copes with and aids the delivery. As we made our way home, we were still reeling. Stephen turned and said, 'How can anyone not believe in a God, when a woman's body is designed in the most amazing way so that a child can be born?'

No humanly designed machine could even attempt the process, but a woman's body can do it naturally. The first stage of labour prepares the body for what is about to happen. The cervix is opened and at the end of this stage the uterus and vagina make one birth canal for the baby to travel down. The textbooks describe an overwhelming urge to push during the second stage, and talk about how this urge can be all-consuming and thrilling. There is no rational decision that this is the best thing to do for yourself and the baby, but it is a primal force that enables you and ends with the delivery of your baby. Somehow a woman's body is able to undertake this process, and afterwards return to its former self. Stephen was right when he said that the design of the body is amazing.

Unless you became a parent by adoption, you or your partner have been through the experience of labour, and you may or may not have felt that your labour was a textbook case. Memories of it are coloured by time, and in Jacqui's case by gas and air, so our recollections of the same births differ. Whatever your experience of labour, the end result is a new life beginning, and that is the most challenging and exciting part of all.

The beginning of today's reading focuses on how God is everywhere. There is nowhere that we can go to escape his presence. There may be times after the birth when all we want to do is to get away from people, from cooing new grandparents or slightly awkward old friends who feel obliged to visit 'the new arrival'. It may be natural to feel like that; after all, the experience of birth and becoming a new parent is a very personal and intimate one, for both the mother and the father. It also takes time to learn how to be a family and so you will need space both alone and with each other. After God created the world he took time off, and we need to as well! It can be tricky to decline the weekend visit from the relatives who think it is their right to pay homage and bring knitted bootees, but it is something many of us need to do if we are to make the best of the precious early days of family life.

However, Psalm 139 reminds us that God himself will not leave us at this time. It speaks of how his 'hand will guide me, (his) right hand will hold me fast' (v. 10). God's protective arm around us will keep us safe, for he is motivated by love for us. 'If I go up to the heavens, you are there; if I make my bed in the depths, you are there,' wrote the psalmist (v. 8). Even 'if I rise on the wings of the dawn' (v. 9), God's presence is there. Most new parents quickly gain experience in rising on the wings of the dawn. This psalm assures us that when we're trying to settle a crying baby at 3 a.m., when we're trying to pick up the pieces of our lives again, when we feel exhausted or defeated, God is present. It may not feel as if he is, but he is.

As the psalm continues, it speaks about how God knows us intimately from the time we were in our mother's womb. He saw us and knew of our existence even before our own parents did. God ultimately designed us, and gave us life.

Similarly, he has been involved in the life of our new child before we were aware of him or her. Quietly, mysteriously, he has brought this new individual into being. Throughout history God has been able to see the child developing. 'My frame was not hidden from you when I was made in the secret place. When I was woven together in the depths of the earth, your eyes saw my unformed body,' says the psalmist (vv. 15–16). Nowadays we also are able to monitor the developing child's progress, through ultrasound. It is an awesome thing to see on a monitor the unborn child, to see the heartbeat and the growing limbs and to know that it is created out of us.

The development of a new life inside a mother is completely mind-blowing. When we become parents, we share first-hand in something of the creative power of God. We as parents are a part of the creation of a new human life from conception, but so is God. When we first become parents, we cannot fail to take a step back from the breath-taking reality of what we have made and to recognize, as God the Creator did, the goodness of this new thing.

**Prayer**

*Heavenly Father, thank you for your life-giving involvement in creation. Thank you that in the birth of our child you allow us to share a part of your creative power. May the wonder of your creation never cease to bring us joy. Thank you that we are fearfully and wonderfully made. Through Jesus Christ our Lord. Amen*

# The gift of a new life

**1 Samuel 1:1–2, 9–20 (NRSV)**

There was a certain man of Ramathaim, a Zuphite from the hill country of Ephraim, whose name was Elkanah son of Jeroham son of Elihu son of Tohu son of Zuph, an Ephraimite. He had two wives; the name of the one was Hannah, and the name of the other Peninnah. Peninnah had children, but Hannah had no children...

After they had eaten and drunk at Shiloh, Hannah rose and presented herself before the Lord. Now Eli the priest was sitting on the seat beside the door-post of the temple of the Lord. She was deeply distressed and prayed to the Lord, and wept bitterly. She made this vow: 'O Lord of hosts, if only you will look on the misery of your servant, and remember me, and not forget your servant, but will give to your servant a male child, then I will set him before you as a nazirite until the day of his death. He shall drink neither wine nor intoxicants, and no razor shall touch his head.'

As she continued praying before the Lord, Eli observed her mouth. Hannah was praying silently; only her lips moved, but her voice was not heard; therefore Eli thought she was drunk. So Eli said to her, 'How long will you make a drunken spectacle of yourself? Put away your wine.' But Hannah answered, 'No, my lord, I am a woman deeply troubled; I have drunk neither wine nor strong drink, but I have been pouring out my soul before the Lord. Do not regard your servant as a worthless woman, for I have been speaking out of my great anxiety and vexation all this time.' Then Eli answered, 'Go in peace; the God of Israel grant the petition you have made to him.' And she said, 'Let your servant find favour in your sight.' Then the woman went to her quarters, ate and drank with her husband, and her countenance was sad no longer.

They rose early in the morning and worshipped before the Lord; then they went back to their house at Ramah. Elkanah knew his wife Hannah, and the Lord remembered her.

In due time Hannah conceived and bore a son. She named him Samuel, for she said, 'I have asked him of the Lord.'

Some people have 'green fingers'. Anything that they plant grows and flowers. House-plants thrive with their care. They have a rapport with nature that is incredible.

Jacqui is not one of those people. Friends buy her cut flowers rather than plants for birthdays as they have a longer life expectancy! It is not through lack of trying on her part. She waters her plants, and carefully tries to locate them somewhere suitable. She has even been known to use one of those little cloths to shine the leaves, but her fingers insist on remaining a colour other than green.

God, by contrast, is green-fingered. In fact, he is the author of all life. He is able to establish and nurture life in plants, animals, us. All life ultimately comes from him.

People have always been involved in God's life-giving work. Through childbirth we share in the wonder of creation. Today's advances in medical science have made it possible for human beings to be involved in that process in new ways. The development of fertility treatments has meant the possibility and reality of children for many couples who were previously considered unable to have them. Before any attempts at such treatments are made, people go through counselling and a prolonged vetting procedure, involving perhaps months of uncertainty and frustration. For most couples wanting a baby, by whatever means, there is a period of trying to conceive, where disappointment has to be faced and overcome. Anyone who has been involved in that process knows that ultimately there is no guarantee of success. We share in God's creative work, but it is he alone who ordains life.

In today's reading, Hannah is desperate to have a child of her own. Here is a woman who has other children around her, but she wants one of her own. She wants to experience life-giving for herself, and being surrounded by another woman's children just emphasizes her own situation. In desperation she turns to God.

At that time, this was her only option—no IVF was available in Old Testament times. Hannah demonstrated to God that she was serious about it. She went out of her way, left her husband celebrating and took herself to the temple. She was determined, she knew what she wanted, and she went and asked. She was not even afraid of making a spectacle of herself, attracting the attention of the priest so that he came over, thinking she was drunk. But she was not drunk.

She was a woman desperate for God to perform a miracle.

When we know someone who seems very confident in themselves, we might say that they think they are 'God's gift'. It's a phrase that we use negatively, implying that this person is not as great as they think they are. But actually, the expression contains more than a grain of truth. Ultimately, whatever the situation, be it Hannah in the Old Testament, or us now, life is always a gift given to us by God. Our child is God's gift to us. But gifts bring challenges and responsibilities too, and sometimes it is only with the passing of time that these become clear.

We mentioned earlier that Jacqui is not 'green-fingered'. (Neither is Stephen, for that matter, but it doesn't much bother him!) For most of our married life, this hasn't been a problem. Our gardens have been so small that the occasional half-hour with a trowel or a mower has been enough to keep things reasonably trim. When we moved to our last house, we inherited a huge garden, completely overgrown with brambles, weeds and nettles from one side to the other. We knew that we had no chance of sorting it all out on our own, so, to begin with, we got an expert in. He was able to clear the main area and put turf down, and give our young children somewhere to play. But after he had gone, the responsibility to build upon what he had done fell on us.

So over the past two years, we have had to learn a bit. At times we have even enjoyed it. The excitement when a bulb that we planted grows, or a seedling takes root, is great. Better still is having a safe place for our children to run and climb and play, and a quiet spot to sit outside on a summer evening. One summer we even held a barbecue for our church to show off all our hard work. The garden may have been a gift that we did not want but as we have lived with it and worked on it, it is a gift we have come to accept and then to appreciate.

We may not be willing to admit it, but sometimes many of us who are parents feel that, if our child is a gift from God, then he or she is a gift we don't altogether want. Some new parents worry that they don't really feel as they should about their baby. They expected to experience overwhelming waves of love which never came. Others know that they love their newborn, but are overawed by the responsibilities and hard work that parenthood brings.

Children are a gift from God, but they may be a gift, like our garden, which we have to learn to appreciate and enjoy. It takes time and effort, and the ability to live with imperfection, to begin to enjoy a child. If the feelings of love aren't there at the beginning, they can come as we invest ourselves into this new life we have been given. During the first weeks and months of parenthood, pressure, tiredness and unsettled hormones may make our feelings very unreliable predictors of the future. In any case, the gifts we like the most when we receive them aren't always the ones we continue to treasure over the years.

In all of this, the key is recognizing our child or children as God's gift to us, and being prepared to go on working even when times are tough. Hannah must have known something of this. She had to live with the heartache of the separation that her vow to God—to dedicate her first-born to him—entailed. She had to deal with changes in the family pecking order, now that both Elkanah's wives were mothers. But she continued to recognize God as the source of Samuel's existence. She realized that her child was a gift from God, and then she helped him to grow up in a way that brought honour to his Creator. She worshipped God for the gift that he had given to her.

**Prayer**

*Lord God, thank you for the gift of life. Today, please help us as we learn more about how to take care of the precious gift you have given us. May we always praise you for what you have given. In Jesus' name. Amen*

# Real life with children

**Proverbs 10:1 (NRSV)**
A wise child makes a glad father, but a foolish child is a mother's grief.

**Proverbs 27:11 (NRSV)**
Be wise, my child, and make my heart glad, so that I may answer whoever reproaches me.

**Proverbs 20:11 (NRSV)**
Even children make themselves known by their acts, by whether what they do is pure and right.

Stephen and I met when we were students. Stephen was studying sociology and I was studying psychology. As we got to know each other, our biases became more evident to each other. Stephen was always looking at the big picture, at how government decisions affected countries and continents. I was much more concerned about individuals and how they were affected. The human-interest story at the end of the news bulletin, when Stephen was ready to switch off, tended to be when I was just becoming interested. Our educational backgrounds were also evident when it came to children as well. As a sociologist, Stephen had been taught that it is society and culture that shape a person's character. As a psychologist, I had understood that people's personalities are genetic, and are fixed at birth. Our two disciplines have traditionally disputed this issue hotly. The so-called nature–nurture debate was at one time a live issue in our home. Experience has mellowed both our views!

When a child is born, it is right that there is excitement and wonder at the new creation that has emerged into the world. However, for the new parents, there can also be an overpowering sense of hard-edged reality. This wonderful creature whom God created and all the grandparents and uncles and aunts adore also has an amazing ability to cry for hours on end, preventing us from ever sitting down for a complete meal without interruption. The endless task of cleaning up baby's waste products from both ends brings us down to earth with a crash, and as a new parent it seems as if we never have any time with our partner, or to ourselves. The dream of 'Grandma's little angel' can all too often feel to us like a nightmare. Whether baby's less appealing characteristics can be attributed to nature or nurture we will leave to the social scientists to resolve, but that these characteristics can take their toll on hard-pressed parents, there is little doubt.

If you do not recognize that description of life with your baby, then be thankful! But if you do, then rest assured that many others have been there before you. I know of no easy way to stem the flow of sick, and I often struggled with having to eat a meal with a baby on my knee. One lesson I learned early on, though, was to accept help when it is offered. Soon after Natalie, our first child, was born, we had a friend staying with us who did not have children of his own. It was teatime and we had just sat down when, as usual, Natalie started to cry. I stood up to get her, but our friend beat me to her, and after that it sometimes became a bit of a race! I found it hard to accept help, even though it was evident to everyone around that I needed it, because of a misplaced sense of duty to my child. Since then, I have been better at accepting the help that is offered, and appreciate the good friends whom God has given me, who have been prepared to help out in times of need.

When we watch the television or read child-care books, we can overdose on images of domestic joy, which at times feel far removed from reality. Thankfully the Bible is more honest. Whilst it affirms that children are indeed a gift from God to be enjoyed, it also shows us some of the struggle and heartache of parenting. This realism is seen through stories of rebellious children, such as David's son Absalom, as well as proverbs such as those in our reading for today. Wise children make for glad parents. Rebellious and foolish ones give their parents grief.

The Proverbs also tell us that even children reveal their nature through their actions. Even from a very young age you can begin to see a child's personality coming through. As a tiny baby, Natalie would get easily upset about things, but would also be easily calmed down and distracted from her tears. As she grows up, this is still very much a central characteristic of hers. Simeon, our second child, was a much more placid baby, but if he got upset over something then drastic measures were needed, and even now, when we think we may have shifted him from his depression he will suddenly start all over again. As a parent, you learn how to deal with your different children. I know to send Stephen in to Simeon when he is in a state, as Stephen stands a better chance of calming him down, in the same way as my mum used to send my dad in to me!

As far as the nature–nurture debate goes, Stephen and I ended up taking the middle ground. There are characteristics that children seem to have from birth, and however much you try to bring them up similarly, they end up unique. However, parents and the child's surroundings also help to make the person they become. The book of Proverbs acknowledges that children are not always perfect, that a child's behaviour even from an early age needs shaping. I am not, of course, suggesting that from the age of several weeks you should start preaching to your child or disciplining him if he cries too much or will not sleep at night. But it is never too early to start praying with your child present, it is never too early to demonstrate your unconditional love for her. From the time of her birth, your behaviour is going to shape your child.

At times the joy and excitement of the new life may be dampened by the hardship and lack of sleep which accompany it. I remember lying in a hospital bed feeling overwhelmed with love and excitement, but then a few days later feeling alone and exhausted, and terrifyingly responsible for the vulnerable life awake and crying in my arms. As it was God who ordained the life of your child, he will also give you the resources to cope with him or her, even when the reality is not all that you may have dreamed about. The first few weeks of a child's life are a huge strain on the parent, as adjustments are made and new relationships are developed. Whether these feelings are for fleeting minutes or longer-term, it is good to turn to God in these times.

**Prayer**

*Dear Lord, today, may I know your peace and be aware of your presence. Thank you that you know me and know my child. Thank you that you love us both, despite knowing us intimately. Give me grace as I strive to be a good parent. Amen*

# From the lips of children

**Psalm 8 (NIV)**

O Lord, our Lord,
how majestic is your name in all the earth!
You have set your glory
above the heavens.
From the lips of children and infants
you have ordained praise
because of your enemies,
to silence the foe and the avenger.
When I consider your heavens,
the work of your fingers,
the moon and the stars,
which you have set in place,
what is man that you are mindful of him,
the son of man that you care for him?
You made him a little lower than the heavenly beings
and crowned him with glory and honour.
You made him ruler over the works of your hands;
you put everything under his feet:
all flocks and herds,
and the beasts of the field,
the birds of the air,
and the fish of the sea, all that swim the paths of the seas.
O Lord, our Lord,
how majestic is your name in all the earth!

**Matthew 21:15–16 (NIV)**

But when the chief priests and the teachers of the law saw the wonderful things he did and the children shouting in the temple area, 'Hosanna to the Son of David,' they were indignant.

'Do you hear what these children are saying?' they asked him.

'Yes,' replied Jesus, 'have you never read, "From the lips of children and infants you have ordained praise"?'

When I was eight years old, I spent a mercifully brief time at a boys' public school of a rather traditional type. Six days a week I trekked off on the train, NHS spectacles peering anxiously out beneath the cap that was the crowning glory of my preposterous uniform. If I had worn a badge saying 'bully me' I could not have looked more vulnerable. In the hours ahead awaited the tortures of rugby and cross-country runs, endless maths and geography tests, and the wearing indignity of being always addressed by one's surname in a teacherly bark which would have been more at home in the military.

One of the things I learned fast was that teachers were there to teach, and I was there to learn. They had the answers, the knowledge my parents were paying for. My mind, in theory at least, was the blank page on which that knowledge was to be reproduced. This was not an environment that encouraged alternative points of view or the questioning of what we were taught. To do so would probably have ended in a trip to the much-feared headmaster's study.

Now, as a minister in the church, I hope I don't make the same mistake, of thinking that I have wisdom and knowledge and that I must pass this on to my congregation. I hope I have learned that my congregation, many of whom have been members of my church since before I was born, have things to teach me too. I hope I am ready to look and to listen and to learn from their wisdom and experience, just as I hope they are ready to learn from what I have to offer them.

Come to that, as a parent, I hope I have learned the same lesson. It is all too easy to regard our children as fresh canvases on which we must paint out of our store of wisdom and insights. We need to realize that they have things to teach us too.

Children can teach us things by accident, without meaning to. When someone in our house is ill, our five-year-old will tell us that we should lay hands on them and pray so that Jesus will make them better. I don't have it in my heart to explain that not everyone is healed when we pray for them, so we do it, and sometimes our simple, childish prayer gets results. In the middle of an argument, one of the children will ask quite innocently why Mummy and Daddy are fighting, and as we try to think of an answer we will realize that we don't know either. When visitors turn up at the front door, unannounced and unexpected, a child may ask all sorts of things about them and their lives, and I realize that I have never bothered to find out about them at all.

Jesus, of course, never had this problem. He knew that children have much to teach us. That is why he held them up as an example to us. He welcomed them even when he was exhausted after a hard day's ministry, refusing to accept his disciples' self-aggrandising protection of him. He taught that anyone who wanted to enter the kingdom of God needed to do so, not full of pride and self-importance, but with wonder and excitement, like a child in a toy shop at Christmas. He remembered and quoted David's psalm when the religious officials wanted the children to follow their example and sit in sombre judgment upon Jesus.

I sometimes wonder whether David loved the idea of God being praised by children and infants because in them he recognized kindred spirits. David was, after all, a worshipper of God first and foremost, before he was king or general. That is why so many of his poems and songs of praise have been preserved for us. There is an extravagance, an unbridledness, about David's worship, and not just when things were going well. Even in the psalms of lament there is a richness and reality which puts most of our worship to shame. It was David who was despised by his wife because he cared more about worshipping the Lord with every fibre of his being than he did about the dignity of his office (2 Samuel 6:16).

Children don't care about dignity. They aren't bothered about looking cool. This, admittedly, ceases to be true some time before adolescence arrives, but young children at least don't try to cover up real emotion for fear of what others will think. The same is true in worship.

Many churches struggle a bit with worship. We mumble into our books songs about our longing to dance before the Lord. As we sing about the joy of knowing God, we look like mourners at a funeral. The children, though, are often an exception. If they know a song or can pick it up, children will dance, sing, shout. Sometimes they need to be calmed down. There is an exuberance about their worship which David relished, and Jesus loved. What a put-down it was to the religious teachers of the day, to say to them, 'While you are looking critically at what God is doing, the children are recognizing it, and celebrating it in worship.'

The chief priests and the teachers of the law were probably not too pleased to be told to learn from the street-children about worship. They were too full of what they knew, confident of their status and power and learning. So what about us? Are we willing to learn from our children, whatever age they may be, however wise we may feel we are? Or are we, like the religious officials of Jesus' time, too satisfied with ourselves to hear what God might be saying to us through them?

**Prayer**

*Lord Jesus, thank you that you understood and recognized what we could learn from children. Please teach us to be more child-like in our appreciation of you, so that we can praise you and worship you with all of our being. May our children always remind us of your love and concern for children, so that we can learn from them too each day. Amen*

# Let the children come

**Mark 10:13–16 (NRSV)**

People were bringing little children to him in order that he might touch them; and the disciples spoke sternly to them. But when Jesus saw this, he was indignant and said to them, 'Let the little children come to me; do not stop them; for it is to such as these that the kingdom of God belongs. Truly I tell you, whoever does not receive the kingdom of God as a little child will never enter it.' And he took them up in his arms, laid his hands on them, and blessed them.

We recently enjoyed a fabulous summer holiday. For three hot August weeks we explored some of the major cities of northern Italy, in particular Venice and Florence. These were cities that the two of us had visited years ago, long before we had children, but not since, and we wondered how our two children would get on with them. The attractions that these cities held for us included museums, architecture, churches, and, I admit, cheap food and wine. None of these are generally regarded as being high on the priority list of young children, but to our relief and surprise, our five- and three-year-old managed very well. Admittedly we occasionally had to resort to bribes, trips to McDonald's and The Disney Store being particular favourites. But for the most part we found that there were details in lots of galleries and churches that could be made intriguing to young minds.

The churches were the most difficult. Many Italian churches greet visitors with a large sign informing them of all the things they are not allowed to do inside. These include talking, taking photos, wearing shorts, eating ice-cream, praying... OK, I made the last one up! Inside these churches, there would usually be a stern-looking man whose job it was to make sure that the rules were rigorously enforced. These characters seemed to be suspicious of visitors in general, and children in particular. So as we queued to get in, we would remind our children of the need, once inside, to be quiet, to stay with Mummy and Daddy, and so on. When occasionally they disobeyed, these guardians of decorum would march over and tell us off in Italian.

The children had difficulty understanding this because their experience of our church is so different. To watch them on a Sunday morning, you would think we had signs up positively encouraging talking, running, and jumping off pews. (We haven't.) 'Why have we got to be quiet?' we were frequently asked.

Most parents have similar experiences, and many of them are closer to home than Venice or Florence. Visiting a church with friends or on holiday, we may notice irritated stares from regulars when our child makes a noise. Even worse, returning to our own church with our new baby, we feel the disapproval from people we have previously felt at home with. In the most extreme of cases we may even encounter the deacon or churchwarden who asks us to keep our child silent or else take him or her out.

Jesus was surrounded by such people. The disciples didn't want children hanging around Jesus. Children didn't know how to behave when in the company of the Messiah. They might cry or pick their noses or need to be taken to the toilet at just the crucial point in his sermon. The older ones might interrupt and ask questions when they didn't understand something he had said. It was far too risky to let them come close to Jesus. Better to allow him to speak to the crowds of more predictable, docile adults, those who knew how to behave.

But Jesus was having none of it. Not only did he welcome and bless them, but he used them to teach the disciples a home truth or two. They thought that they controlled access to Jesus, that in some sense his Kingdom belonged to them. 'No,' says Jesus. 'My Kingdom doesn't belong to the petty-minded officials, the "jobs-worths" of this world. It doesn't belong to you. It belongs to these children, and those who come to me as they do.'

Have you ever wondered where the real teaching gets done in our churches? During the sermon, the adults sit quietly, apparently attentive. They know better than to interrupt when the vicar is in full flow. After the service, there may be the occasional comment of 'Nice sermon today' or some such, but rarely any real discussion or disagreement. Meanwhile, in the Junior Church, children who have not been taught to sit in silence ask questions, often impossible ones, and tell their leader why she is wrong about something. But when they believe, they really do believe, and when they learn to love Jesus, they do so with a freshness that puts many of us to shame. It is clear why Jesus told us to come to him as a child does.

So what are we to do if we find, after we have children, that the church which has been our spiritual home actually has more in common with the closed mindset of the disciples or the Italian church officials than with the open, welcoming attitude of Jesus?

The first thing we might need to do is to change churches. This is not a flippant suggestion. When we start a family we change, and our needs change, and it may be that the church which has been so helpful to us in the previous period of our life is no longer the best place for us. It may be time to move on, to a fellowship where all members of the church, regardless of age, are welcomed and accepted. Children who grow up feeling that the church does not want them may decide as adults that they don't want it either.

Secondly, we might need to examine our own attitudes. Have we also exhibited an intolerant or unwelcoming attitude to others? We may not have disapproved of children, but of the person with learning difficulties who is sometimes noisy in the service, or the lady who sits in the row behind and sings loudly and out of tune. Perhaps the first step to changing the attitude of the church is to change our own attitude.

Finally, whatever our church might be like, we need to ensure that our children grow up knowing that they are special to God, knowing that they are loved by him, and knowing that they are part of his family as well as ours. That way, when they pick up contradictory signals from others in the church, they will be able to rise above them, because of their security in the love of God.

**Prayer**

*Dear Lord Jesus, thank you that you welcomed children into your presence, and that you overruled your disciples when they tried to protect you from the disruption that children bring. Please help our children always to know that they are special to you. Help us in our church to welcome and accept all sorts of people, and not to be defensive on your behalf. Amen*

# Stumbling-blocks

**Matthew 18:1–6 (NRSV)**

At that time the disciples came to Jesus and asked, 'Who is the greatest in the kingdom of heaven?' He called a child, whom he put among them, and said, 'Truly I tell you, unless you change and become like children, you will never enter the kingdom of heaven. Whoever becomes humble like this child is the greatest in the kingdom of heaven. Whoever welcomes one such child in my name welcomes me.

'If any of you put a stumbling-block before one of these little ones who believe in me, it would be better for you if a great millstone were fastened around your neck and you were drowned in the depth of the sea.'

Under the heading of 'New Life' we have been looking at some of the implications of welcoming a new son or daughter into our family. Some of us may have felt we were fairly well prepared for the adjustments this new addition forces upon us. Most of us, though, are caught by surprise by the extent of the changes, especially when our first child is born. Before we had children, friends told us that starting a family is a far more dramatic change in lifestyle than getting married, and we secretly doubted their word, but in fact experience has borne out this assertion. Because so much of the preparation time that pregnancy gives us gets used up with preparing for labour and birth itself, we may have found ourselves feeling frighteningly unprepared for the first days and weeks of parenthood. Some of our readings and comments under 'New Life' have been designed to help us reflect on this, to allow the Bible to address some of our feelings about it, and to help us bring those feelings to God.

In the last couple of readings in particular, we saw how Jesus not only welcomed and loved children, but held them up as an example to his followers, and some of this is going on in our reading today. But there is also another dimension, a stern note of warning, to which we shall return later on.

We once knew a man for whom the whole idea of serving God in the church was about status and prestige. He hoped he might become a vicar someday, and he would happily describe his ordination as he anticipated it would be. In his imagination, he was the centre of attention, robed up to the nines, with friends and strangers alike suitably impressed and humbled before him. He was sure he would achieve high office in the church, and loved to tell others how important he was going to be. In the event, he was never ordained, as far as I am aware.

The disciples were similarly preoccupied with questions of power and prestige. Basking in the reflected glory of Jesus, they loved to debate who was the most important, who was going to sit at Jesus' right hand in his kingdom, and so on. Time after time, Jesus had to try to explain to them that they had missed the point. His kingdom was one in which those ideals of status and significance, so important in this world, were entirely turned on their heads. As so often, he used a child to illustrate his point.

It isn't the great and the good, those who have worth and honour in their own eyes, who are close to the kingdom, says Jesus, but those who are humble, like a child.

Those of us who are parents may wonder how Jesus came to choose a child as a model of humility. Arguments about status and value rage in our house, as amongst the disciples. 'Mummy, which one of us do you love most?' one of our children asks. A futile, tearful argument breaks out about who is the oldest, or the tallest, even though these are simple matters of fact. One child throws a tantrum because the other has been the centre of parental attention for too long. Children are hardly immune from the kind of debates that preoccupied the disciples.

But perhaps the point is that, whatever claims a child may make about his importance, we don't take them very seriously. A child may insist that she has special significance, but everyone knows she is still only a child. In fact, even in those rare cases where such claims may be true, adults are disinclined to take them too seriously. Presumably those who teach Princes William and Harry do not treat them any differently to their classmates. Jesus' parents, with their dawning appreciation of who he was, were still less than pleased to find him debating theology with the grown-ups when he should have been on his way back home with them. It is hard for us to see a child as anything other than a child. We hope that those childish arguments about who is biggest or fastest or cleverest will be set aside with the other things of childhood as the child becomes an adult.

This passage also has a note of warning which we haven't heard before. To welcome a child is to welcome Jesus, but to cause a child to stumble is to incur God's anger.

We live in a time when there is perhaps more awareness than ever before of how adults can cause hurt and damage to children. We now know that child abuse of various types, once seen as rare, affects huge numbers of children, and continues to do so even after they become adults. Debates rage about other ways in which adults may harm children, through exposing them to cigarette smoke or violent television programmes. In a recent case before the European Court of Human Rights, a boy won damages from his stepfather for trauma caused by severe corporal punishments. Everywhere the damaging effects of toxic parenting are being exposed.

This may make for a frightening environment in which to bring up children. We may expose our children to none of these things, yet we know that our parenting mistakes may cause hurt too. We try to avoid being negligent or over-protective, too strict or not strict enough. Could these things be the stumbling-blocks that Jesus talks about?

If we look back at the Bible reading, we see that Jesus is talking about the way in which people come to him. In that context, the stumbling-blocks are quite specifically obstacles to children coming to know and love him. Jesus warns us not that our every parenting mistake is going to damage our child irreversibly, but that we must not cause a child to doubt the love or acceptance of God because of what we say or do.

The best way our children can experience something of God's love is through us. Our unconditional love of them will reflect how God loves them. So it is vital that we do not abuse that relationship through our words or actions. This doesn't mean that there is no place for discipline and correction as our children grow older. Appropriately applied, these are an expression of love, not its opposite. God disciplines us out of his love for us and we should do the same with our children. But even more important, our lives need to demonstrate to our children our fundamental love and acceptance of them, and God's love and acceptance of them, so that they can grow up with that as their experience. When our children know that we love them and believe in them, our relationships with them will be strong enough to cope with the mistakes we all make as parents, so that those mistakes do not become stumbling-blocks for them.

**Prayer**

*Father God, thank you that you have trusted us with the care of children. Please help us, by our love and acceptance of them, to reflect your love and acceptance of them, so that they might grow up knowing that they are cherished and cared for by you. Amen*

# Common-sense parenting

**Colossians 3:21 (NRSV)**
Fathers, do not provoke your children, or they may lose heart.

**Ephesians 6:4 (NRSV)**
And, fathers, do not provoke your children to anger, but bring them up in the discipline and instruction of the Lord.

**Luke 2:39–40 (NRSV)**
When they had finished everything required by the law of the Lord, they returned to Galilee, to their own town of Nazareth. The child grew and became strong, filled with wisdom; and the favour of God was upon him.

Over the next few readings, we are going to look at some of the new responsibilities that a new parent faces, and try to learn from what the Bible teaches us about parenting.

The apostle Paul in his letters would generally balance a command to one party in a relationship with a command to the other party. So instructions to slaves are followed by instructions to masters, teaching to wives balanced by teaching to husbands. It is like that here. In Colossians 3, immediately after Paul instructs children to obey their parents, he goes on to tell parents not to provoke their children.

What does it mean to provoke our children? It surely does not mean anything we do as parents which upsets or angers them, whether that is turning off the television or insisting they eat their vegetables at tea-time. But it may mean anything that leaves them struggling to know what we require of them, or unsure of how we are going to respond to them.

Perhaps the most important way we can avoid doing this is by being consistent with them. When we are consistent in how we bring up our children, they know where they stand with us. They know that our love for them is constant and predictable, as are our expectations of them. But when a parent allows a certain behaviour one day and clamps down on that same behaviour the next, or is very loving and affectionate one day and cold and distant the next, the child receives mixed signals. They may become insecure, confused, angry, feeling misunderstood. Most of us have known children who have been brought up like that, and it is true, as Paul says, that they often lose heart. All of us need to know where we stand in our adult experiences of work and relationships. Common sense tells us that children, who are only beginning to find out about the world around them, need nothing less.

The parallel passage to the Colossians verse, in Ephesians 6, adds a positive command to the negative one. Parents are not only to avoid provoking their children (provoking them 'to anger' in Ephesians) but are also to bring them up 'in the discipline and instruction of the Lord'. We need to give them the security and stability of knowing what we require of them, and knowing what God requires of them, as far as we ourselves understand it.

That doesn't mean that we are to become heavy-handed or dictatorial with our children. There is a difficult balance that we need to strive for as parents between guiding our children and allowing them to learn by their mistakes. We need to learn when to correct and discipline, and when to let something go unchallenged. Parents will find their own place to draw this line, and the needs of each child may mean that the balance has to be slightly different with each one. Of course, when the child is very young this is not an issue, but even then we have to make decisions about how to react. In particular, parents of very young children handle the whole issue of crying very differently. Some will refuse to leave a child to cry for a moment longer than it takes to pick him up. Others will allow their child to cry herself to sleep without a second thought.

When our eldest child Natalie was born, as her mother I felt that it was my responsibility to stop her crying as soon as she began. If I had put her down to sleep, then at the first whimper I was back, holding her, comforting her, feeding her, anything to stop the noise. The trouble was, I could not always stop it! Before long, however, I began to recognize the different cries that Natalie made, those when she really was hungry or wet, and those when she just wanted us to know she was there. I began to know when I needed to do something and when I didn't. It helped: I was less on edge, and less tired, and able to respond to her needs better. It meant I didn't have to leap up at the first cry every time. (Twins and second or later children have to become used to sharing their parents from the start and it does not seem to do them much harm!) Other parents find a way of responding which may be different from mine, but which is right for them and their child. You need to get to know your own child and understand what he is telling you through his cries.

As children grow up, they very quickly learn how to test your boundaries. They want to know what they may and may not do, and they begin to try out new things. One piece of advice which I have found invaluable as a parent is to choose your battles carefully. There are always going to be areas in life where you want your child to do one thing, and they want to do another. You cannot make a big deal out of each and every one of them, but also you cannot let your child, no matter what age, dominate and control everything that you do. This is as true for the toddler who never lets his parent have a conversation with someone else, as for a teenager with her 'attitude'. So as your baby grows, you have to decide what is really important and make sure that you win those battles!

Only you can decide which things you are going to insist on. Most parents would agree that things which are potentially dangerous to their children or to others (for example, playing with electric switches, running into roads) are a definite 'no'. On other issues, parents will differ. Here again, our common sense, the advice of other more experienced parents and the teaching of the Bible are our most useful resources.

When you adopt this attitude, your children will learn for themselves, but they will also know the boundaries that you have established for their good. Over time they should get to know which issues you are not going to back down over, and which there is some flexibility about. This will also mean that at times you feel free to let things drop, knowing that some issues are not really that important. It is a very difficult balance to keep and all parents at times struggle with it, but parenting was never going to be a piece of cake! The most important thing is finding the way of handling it that works for you and your family.

In the short passage from Luke 2, we read that Mary and Joseph did everything that was required for Jesus, and that Jesus grew in strength and wisdom. The requirements of the law that Mary and Joseph obeyed were the ceremonial requirements of circumcision and sacrifice, rather different from anything which we as parents might do for our children today in baptism or dedication. But we might just as easily understand this to be about providing all that is required in love and guidance and security for a child to grow. As we seek to apply the teaching of scripture in our parenting, and look to God for his help and strength in our failings, so we too should have the joy of watching our child grow physically, in maturity of character, and in faith.

**Prayer**

*Heavenly Father, please give us wisdom in how to bring up our child. Help us to be consistent parents, and to provide stability and security for our child. Help us not to provoke our child, but to bring him or her up in your way. In Jesus' name. Amen*

# Learning by example

**2 Chronicles 17:3–4 (NIV)**

The Lord was with Jehoshaphat because in his early years he walked in the ways that his father David had followed. He did not consult the Baals but sought the God of his father and followed his commands rather than the practices of Israel.

**2 Chronicles 22:2–4 (NIV)**

Ahaziah was twenty-two years old when he became king, and he reigned in Jerusalem for one year. His mother's name was Athaliah, a granddaughter of Omri. He too walked in the ways of the house of Ahab, for his mother encouraged him in doing wrong. He did evil in the eyes of the Lord, as the house of Ahab had done, for after his father's death they became his advisers, to his undoing.

In the original trilogy of *Star Wars* films, Luke Skywalker leads the Rebel Alliance in its struggle to liberate the galaxy from the rule of the remote Emperor and his evil henchman, Darth Vader. Skywalker is inspired by the example of his mentor and father-figure, Obi-Wan Kenobi, who sacrifices his own life to save those of his comrades halfway through the first film. Kenobi is a Jedi Knight, someone who has learned to use the power of the mysterious Force for good. But as Luke trains to develop his own Jedi skills, he becomes frighteningly aware of the attraction that the dark side of the Force has for him. The crisis point in Luke's own journey comes when it is revealed in the second film, *The Empire Strikes Back*, that Darth Vader is in fact Luke's own father, a former Jedi himself who found the appeal of the dark side too strong to resist. Luke has to choose between following his father-figure Kenobi into the battle for good, or submitting to the urge to join his biological father in the oppressive world of the Empire.

Luke's struggle is, in part anyway, a consequence of the influence that both characters wield over him, for good or for evil. Experience and common sense tell us that parents and other significant figures powerfully affect the people we grow up to be. We may have set out to be like someone. We may have set out to be the opposite of someone. Either way, who we are has been shaped by how we have reacted to other people, especially our parents, and how their behaviour and the consequences of it have affected our lives.

This is not only, or even mainly, to do with teaching and instruction. Far more powerful than what we say to our children is what we do in front of them. Statistics tell us that children of people who smoke cigarettes are more likely to grow up to be smokers themselves. Probably many of those parents, addicted to nicotine, have pleaded with their children not to take up their habit, yet the words are less powerful than the example. Many children, when asked what they want to do for a living when they grow up, will automatically respond with Mummy or Daddy's profession. Whilst the desire to follow the same career as our parents dissipates in most of us, as we discover our own interests and abilities, the desire to copy at least those aspects of our parents which we most admired remains. Luke Skywalker's problem is essentially that he has one too many father-figures, and they are in conflict with each other.

The Bible, as ever, is very realistic when it comes to the influence of parental example. The Old Testament histories in particular regularly tell us how a king followed in the ways of his father, for good or for ill, and got what was coming to him as a result. We have read two such examples today. God was with Jehoshaphat because, in his earlier years at least, he followed in the footsteps of his predecessor David and his father Asa, commended in 2 Chronicles 14:2 as a king who did what was right in God's sight. In particular, Jehoshaphat seems to have been committed to the worship of the one true God, and to have had a hatred of false religion and idolatry—characteristics of all those kings who are remembered positively in the Old Testament.

On the other hand, Ahaziah, the subject of our second reading, is one of the least-remembered, most unfortunate kings of the Old Testament. Made king when barely in his twenties because he was the only surviving male of his family, his reign lasted only a year before he was assassinated. He is recorded as one who 'did evil in the eyes of the Lord' (2 Chronicles 22:4) under the influence of his mother and the traditions of his dynasty, and who suffered the consequences of it.

We are unlikely to be rearing future monarchs (unless this book is being read in high places!) but the example we set our children is just as important. So what are my children learning from my example? Are they learning to be caring towards other people, or to criticize people behind their backs? Are they learning to be ill-tempered or good-humoured? Are they learning to be anxious about the future, or to trust in God's provision? Are they learning to be true to their word, or to make promises they won't keep?

Whatever we teach our children verbally, our actions are the things which will influence them most. Ask yourself today whether you are teaching your child by your actions lessons it would be better for him not to learn. If your child grows up to 'walk in your ways', to borrow the language of our readings, will she be following the commandments of the Lord, or doing evil in his sight? Do you hope your child copies what he sees in you, or do you hope and pray that he doesn't?

As a new parent, you have the opportunity to reconsider why or how you do things. The prospect of influencing our children for good rather than in bad ways may give us the motivation that we need to give up bad habits, with perhaps better odds on success than for New Year's resolutions! The decisions that you make about how you behave in front of your children will affect how they turn out. (Decisions that you make about how you behave when they are *not* around are bound to have some effect on them too!) It is worth thinking about and praying about this issue alone and with your partner, even from this early stage of your child's life. The example we set today will influence the lives our children lead tomorrow.

**Prayer**

*Dear Lord, thank you for those whose good example has helped us to be the people we are today. Please help us to teach our child to follow in your ways, not only by the things we say, but also by the things we do. Amen*

# Teachers and trainers

**Proverbs 22:6 (NIV)**

Train a child in the way he should go, and when he is old he will not turn from it.

**Psalm 34:11–16 (NIV)**

Come, my children, listen to me;
    I will teach you the fear of the Lord.
Whoever of you loves life
    and desires to see many good days,
keep your tongue from evil
    and your lips from speaking lies.
Turn from evil and do good;
    seek peace and pursue it.
The eyes of the Lord are on the righteous
    and his ears are attentive to their cry;
the face of the Lord is against those who do evil,
    to cut off the memory of them from the earth.

In the previous reading, we thought about how our children are shaped and influenced by us, in particular by the example we set. In the reading before that we began to look at what the Bible says about the new responsibilities we face as parents, and thought about the importance of consistency and common sense in our parenting. Today we look more specifically at the importance of training and teaching our children.

We live in a society which attaches great importance to teaching and training. All children between the ages of five and sixteen are required to be in school full-time, and increasing numbers of people begin formal education before that time, in nursery school, or continue it in sixth form, college or university. Tony Blair, the UK's Labour Prime Minister, is on record as saying that the three chief priorities of his government are 'education, education, education'. The nature and quality of the education our children receive, and the ways this can be evaluated, are issues of vital importance for many parents. Some families move from one area to another in order to get their children into apparently more successful schools. Others spend vast sums to educate their children privately. Any contemporary moral debate, for example about drugs or sex, always emphasizes the role of the education system in training and shaping our children.

The Bible also emphasizes the importance of teaching children. In fact, there are far more verses about children's need for training and instruction than there are about their need for love and attention. But the Bible's commands here are directed at parents, not the Secretary of State for Education.

Some parents, Christian and otherwise, choose to remove their children from collective education, and teach them at home themselves. Most of us will feel that the losses involved in this—not being part of a school community, forgoing the expertise of trained teachers—outweigh the benefits. But it is vital that we as parents don't imagine that our state education system relieves us altogether of our duty to teach.

As the vicar of an Anglican church, Stephen is quite often asked by parents to write references for their children to support their applications to Church of England schools. Sometimes he asks why the parents feel that a church school is the best thing for their child. Often they respond, 'We want young Jo(e) to get a good grounding in Christian moral values.' This is laudable, but it is a problem if parents believe that the school can do that single-handed. The best church school in the world can only back up and reinforce what is being taught at home. If we imagine that our teachers, often with over thirty children to a class, and with the demands of the National Curriculum to fulfil, are able to provide the foundational teaching in Christian living that is lacking at home, then we are in for a shock when our children grow up.

Proverbs 22:6 reminds us of the purpose of training. Good teaching doesn't just fill our minds with facts and instructions. Rather, it shapes us. It makes us who we are. We may not remember very much of what we learned at school, but we may remember the one or two teachers who exercised a real influence on us. They may well have been the ones who gave us space to explore and express ourselves, not the ones who were only concerned with transferring information from their brains to ours. Similarly, we may not remember lots of the things that we were told to do and not to do by our parents when we were children, but we can see the effects of their teaching in the way we live now. That is why children who have been well trained are likely to continue in the same way. Not because they have lots of instructions in their minds to which they can refer, but because they have been shaped by the trainer.

So, as we seek to train our children, we need to remember that it isn't just about telling them what to do or what not to do. For very young children, that doesn't work anyway. Instead it is about what we encourage, about the values we model in our own lives and explain to them. It is about the times we affirm something they have done, and the times we express disapproval, ideally with some explanation of why we disapprove. It is about the stories we tell them, from the Bible and elsewhere, that form their imagination, that give them heroes to admire and achievements to which they can aspire.

So what should we be attempting to teach our children? As ever, the Psalms and Proverbs have an earthy, practical wisdom to offer. Psalm 34, for instance, tells us to train our children to be careful in their speech, to do good and to seek peace. All of these things, and more, are rooted in the 'fear of the Lord' with which this reading begins. This 'fear' isn't like the terror we might feel at the thought of an intruder in our home, or the illness of a loved one, or the loss of a job. It is rather the deep awe and respect that come from a recognition that God is Creator, that we are his creatures, and that he has designed us and the world for his pleasure and glory. When we understand this, it is natural to seek to live in a way that works with and not against the grain of God's creation. This 'fear of the Lord' is not only the beginning of all wisdom, as the Bible says elsewhere, but of all right living. It is this 'fear' that we should be attempting to instil in our children, by our words and our example. It is this 'fear' that is the foundation of a godly life.

**Prayer**

*Dear Father, we thank you for those people who have taught and trained us, and made us the people we are today. We thank you especially for those who have taught us to love and follow you. We pray that we may train our children to recognize you as their Creator and Lord, and to walk in your ways. Amen*

# Hard love

**Hebrews 12:5–11 (NRSV)**

And you have forgotten the exhortation that addresses you as children—'My child, do not regard lightly the discipline of the Lord, or lose heart when you are punished by him; for the Lord disciplines those whom he loves, and chastises every child whom he accepts.' Endure trials for the sake of discipline. God is treating you as children; for what child is there whom a parent does not discipline? If you do not have that discipline in which all children share, then you are illegitimate and not his children. Moreover, we had human parents to discipline us, and we respected them. Should we not be even more willing to be subject to the Father of spirits and live? For they disciplined us for a short time as seemed best to them, but he disciplines us for our good, in order that we may share his holiness. Now, discipline always seems painful rather than pleasant at the time, but later it yields the peaceful fruit of righteousness to those who have been trained by it.

In the current climate, discipline is a bit of a taboo issue. The trend of allowing every person to express his or her individuality makes us all nervous to give advice or to reprimand, even when the person concerned is a young child. Although being allowed to discover things for ourselves is a good way to learn—and that includes having the freedom to make mistakes—to lead a balanced life, we need to know the boundaries of acceptable behaviour, within which we then have to function and learn. With a young child, you need to establish the boundaries, and at an early age that is all that discipline needs to be about.

Stephen is a great lover of music. His hi-fi and record collection have always been his pride and joy. When we first had children, friends and family alike assumed that the hi-fi system would have to be put out of reach of the children to protect it from inquisitive little fingers. We were determined that although our house should be child-friendly, it would not be completely child-dominated. The hi-fi stayed in place and the children were told 'no' when they went too close to the unit. We had one or two scary moments, but in time the children learned that it was off limits and could be left safely in the room with the hi-fi. Learning and knowing the boundaries of what is and is not acceptable behaviour does lead to a much happier and healthier family life. Stephen still gets to listen to his music and, as a family, music has become an important part of our life together.

This passage in Hebrews shows us God's supreme example of parenting. Verse 6 tells us that the Lord disciplines those he loves, and this is a vital part of parenting. Discipline like this is born out of our love for our child. We need love and discipline for practical parenting, and they need each other to be effective and real. A soft love without discipline will lead to heartache and problems, as the child will be used to doing exactly what he wants when he wants, and at some stage someone is going to have to say 'no' to him. Discipline without love is likely to be unnecessarily harsh, and not motivated by a desire to do what is best for the child. It is a hard love that we need, which truly longs for the best for our children, and is prepared where necessary to discipline to achieve that goal.

The passage goes on to say that if we are not disciplined then we are illegitimate children. From this we can see that it is the duty of every parent to discipline his or her children. It is not an optional extra, but a necessity. As a new parent, this means that you need to teach your child the difference between acceptable and unacceptable behaviour. The rules that you establish for your family are up to you and your partner together as parents. To have one strict parent and one 'laid-back' parent does not work and leads to tension within the marriage relationship as well as the family dynamics. Together you need to work out and enforce the limits of what is and is not acceptable. It is not always easy to agree, and the situation may regularly need reviewing, but as a couple your basic principles of what is and is not allowed need to be constant. In our experience, I can honestly say that when the children know the ground rules, it does make them happier. Of course they will try to flout them at times. The 'terrible twos' can be a dreadful reality as toddlers test and retest the boundaries, but if the rules are there from the beginning, children are more likely to respond to them later on. I have a friend who regularly tells me, 'If you cannot get a three-year-old to listen to you, what chance have you with a teenager?' I find this quite scary, but it is most probably true. One thing I do know is that it is much easier to relax rules than it is to tighten them up at a later stage.

The writer to the Hebrews acknowledges that discipline is not pleasant at the time. As parents, we discover that to be true, not only when we are on the receiving end, but also when we are doing the disciplining. It may not be true to say, 'This is going to hurt me as much as it hurts you', but reprimanding a disobedient child can be emotionally painful and hard.

We are disciplined and moulded by our heavenly Father, and it is in his model that we should discipline and mould our children. God gives us the ideal model of how this should be done, in perfect love and to develop us to our full potential. As human parents, we will sometimes get it wrong. Our own frustrations and agendas can easily come into play when we are dealing with our children, but we need to learn to discipline justly, as we are disciplined by our heavenly Father. God gives us authority over our children, to teach and guide them in his ways, but he has authority over us and we are answerable to him for the way in which we bring up our children. At the end of the passage in Hebrews we are reminded why we should do it. 'Discipline always seems painful rather than pleasant at the time, but later it yields the peaceful fruit of righteousness to those who have been trained by it' (Hebrews 12:11).

**Prayer**

*Heavenly Father, thank you that you guide and discipline us out of love. Teach us how to guide and discipline our child, so that (s)he will grow up with a wise understanding of what is right and wrong. In Jesus' name. Amen*

# Family histories

**Deuteronomy 6:6–7 (NRSV)**

Keep these words that I am commanding you today in your heart. Recite them to your children and talk about them when you are at home and when you are away, when you lie down and when you rise.

**2 Timothy 3:14–15 (NRSV)**

But as for you, continue in what you have learned and firmly believed, knowing from whom you learned it, and how from childhood you have known the sacred writings that are able to instruct you for salvation through faith in Christ Jesus.

Most families have legends that get passed down the generations. We grow up hearing the stories about Great-Uncle Eric who never worked a day in his life yet always had plenty of money, or Great-Grandma who was the first woman bus conductor in town. Often these stories are told to make a moral point. 'Have courage and you'll succeed like your Grandpa.' 'If you don't start saving for the future you'll end up like your Auntie.' These stories give us a sense of belonging to a family with a shared history which helps to make us what we are. Sometimes we feel we know these relatives, who may have died before we were born, better than we know some of our family members who are still living. This may be the case particularly when others see something of our predecessors in us. As a child, Stephen was regularly told how he took after his grandfather, whom he barely knew. As a result, Stephen feels he knows his grandfather better than he does other relations with whom he has spent far more time.

In other cultures, far more importance is attached to passing down these tales of the family and community than is the case here in the individualistic West. Stories of ancestors and their exploits, of heroes and kings, battles won and battles lost, explain the way things are now and give a sense of belonging to a particular community with its own history, roots and identity. The Old Testament goes in for this kind of story-telling in a big way. But these stories are not just the records of a family or a people. They are the stories of a covenant relationship between God and his chosen people. Whether explicitly the focus of the story, or woven into the fabric of it, God is always the subject of it.

These are the stories which were to be recited, passed on and memorized by each new generation. They were to be transmitted in such a way that they became the backdrop against which life was lived, the world-view through which lived experience was to be understood.

As stories of Abraham and Moses, the Exodus and Mount Sinai, and later on of David and Solomon, were passed down through the generations, so each new generation came to see itself in relation to those who had gone before, and in relation to the God who had made covenant with their ancestors.

These stories always had a profoundly moral aspect to them, for they were stories not only about people who had lived long ago, but also about their relationship with God. At the heart of this relationship was the Law of the Old Testament, given to Moses. It was the Law, above all else, which was to be passed on, memorized and taken to heart. So this story not only told its hearers who they were and where they had come from, but also how to live in the present.

It's never too early to start telling these stories to our children. It is said that we learn most in the first five years of our lives, yet our education system does not begin until our children are around five years old. Many of us parents similarly do not start consciously to tell our children their stories and ours until we are sure they are old enough to understand. Yet understanding is only part of it. As we tell the stories that make our children who they are, even before they can clearly comprehend each detail, we give them the raw material on which they will later reflect at a time when they are able to do so. We are furnishing their imagination.

For us as Christians, these stories will not only be about relatives and ancestors, but also about our wider family, the 'household of faith'. We will tell the gospel story, the story of God's dealings with us and the world. As our children grow to experience this as their own story, they become a part of it, and it of them.

Paul referred Timothy back to the faith that he had learned as a child. From older relatives, he had heard stories of the people of God from the patriarchs to his own time. He had heard stories of God's dealings with the world. Most of all, he had heard stories of Jesus. Those stories had become part of who he was. They had become his story, too. On this foundation was Timothy's adult faith built.

For our children, too, the stories that we tell them, and seek to live by ourselves, can be the bedrock of adult faith, as the story of God's dealings with the world become for them the history of their own community, and their stories are caught up into God's story.

**Prayer**

*Heavenly Father, thank you for the story of my family, which has helped to make me who I am. Thank you, too, that you have made my story part of that great story of your family. Please help me as I seek to teach my child that great story, so that (s)he may have a firm foundation for adult faith. In Jesus' name. Amen*

# When all you want to do is hide!

**Judges 6:11–16 (NRSV)**

Now the angel of the Lord came and sat under the oak at Ophrah, which belonged to Joash the Abiezrite, as his son Gideon was beating out wheat in the wine press, to hide it from the Midianites. The angel of the Lord appeared to him and said to him, 'The Lord is with you, you mighty warrior.' Gideon answered him, 'But sir, if the Lord is with us, why then has all this happened to us? And where are all his wonderful deeds that our ancestors recounted to us, saying, "Did not the Lord bring us up from Egypt?" But now the Lord has cast us off, and given us into the hand of Midian.' Then the Lord turned to him and said, 'Go in this might of yours and deliver Israel from the hand of Midian; I hereby commission you.' He responded, 'But sir, how can I deliver Israel? My clan is the weakest in Manasseh, and I am the least in my family.' The Lord said to him, 'But I will be with you, and you shall strike down the Midianites, every one of them.'

At the beginning of this section, we are going to be looking at the story of Gideon as an introduction to several readings about the different challenges that we face as new parents.

Gideon was not having a good day. He was, in a cowardly way, secretly trying to thresh wheat in the confines of a wine press where he would not be discovered. He was feeling small and wanting to hide when, all of a sudden, some joker greets him as a 'mighty warrior'! Maybe, as he has been threshing, he has been thinking about the troubles facing the Israelites at that time, because in response to the stranger's greeting he questions whether the Lord could possibly be with his people while they were being attacked and beaten by their enemies. However, Gideon's visitor is going to acknowledge not only that something needs to be done about the situation, but that Gideon is the man to do it. No more skulking and hiding for Gideon. If his people are going to be free, then he is the one who needs to take action.

It is possible that Gideon's bad day had just got worse. Sometimes it is quite reassuring to have a bit of a moan about how hard life is, and how impossible our situation. Moaning can be a good way of getting something out of our system, particularly if we are tired and feel that we are struggling to cope. For many of us, this is definitely not the time we want someone to come and say to us, 'It is *you* who can make a difference here and now. In fact, God is counting on you.' But that is just what happened to Gideon.

Few of us have experienced angels calling us into battle. But the story of Gideon is helpful when we have to face any new challenge for which we feel unqualified and unprepared, because it reminds us that God is so much bigger than us, our abilities and the situations in which we find ourselves. It also shows us how God equips us for the tasks to which he calls us, even though nothing in our lives so far may have suggested that we have any of the right qualities. We may see ourselves as weak and small, and unable to cope with the challenges we face. God sees us as we can be, in his strength and power, and calls us to fulfil our potential in him.

I remember going on holiday when I was about six months pregnant with Natalie, our first child. I had just left my job, and we were having our last child-free break. As we drove around windy mountain roads in southern Spain, we discussed what life would be like with a new baby, and I was struck with the awful realization that I had no experience of dealing with a child, and absolutely no idea of how I was going to cope. Somehow, though, when Natalie was born I found that many of the most important skills came very naturally. Other things admittedly took some work, and some I never really mastered. But what I did quickly learn was my own dependence on God.

When we become parents, we may feel unqualified and unprepared for what lies ahead. We have had up to nine months to get used to the idea that we are going to have a baby. We may be used to other people's children, nephews and nieces, or we may have worked with young children. We may even have 'borrowed' a baby from a friend to see how we got on, but there is nothing that can fully prepare you for the 24-hour job of being the mother or the father of a new baby. Nothing can equal the joys and frustrations that it brings. So as we face the new challenges of being a parent, like Gideon, what we need most of all is the assurance that God will be with us in the days and weeks ahead, that God will equip us for the task.

Today we have read about Gideon's faltering start at becoming a great warrior for God. As the story progresses, Gideon demands signs and miracles from God before he is willing to trust him and do what God requires of him. It is to be hoped that we will not request as many signs from God as we have to face up to the challenges of parenthood. However, God will be as faithful to us in his provision and support as he was to Gideon when he called him to save the people of Israel.

There will be difficulties and uncertainties as our lives and relationships change and we develop as parents. We will have to face up to challenges and situations which we never expected and for which we feel unprepared and unqualified. We will have to make decisions and live with the consequences of those decisions. Like Gideon, we may feel daunted by the prospect of what lies ahead for us but, as with Gideon, it is God who has called us to the task and it is God who will strengthen us and enable us to complete it. Our calling to be parents may not have been as dramatic as Gideon's to lead his people, and our task not so specific, but the God who gave us the child is the same God who proved his faithfulness to Gideon.

**Prayer**

*Dear Lord, when we feel small and want to hide, please help us to remember that you are bigger than our situation. Give us the strength to cope day by day with the added challenge of being new parents. Amen*

# When all is stripped away

**Judges 7:1–8 (NRSV)**

Then Jerubbaal (that is, Gideon) and all the troops that were with him rose early and encamped beside the spring of Harod; and the camp of Midian was north of them, below the hill of Moreh, in the valley.

The Lord said to Gideon, 'The troops with you are too many for me to give the Midianites into their hand. Israel would only take the credit away from me, saying, "My own hand has delivered me." Now therefore proclaim this in the hearing of the troops, "Whoever is fearful and trembling, let him return home."' Thus Gideon sifted them out; twenty-two thousand returned, and ten thousand remained.

Then the Lord said to Gideon, 'The troops are still too many; take them down to the water and I will sift them out for you there. When I say, "This one shall go with you," he shall go with you; and when I say, "This one shall not go with you," he shall not go.' So he brought the troops down to the water; and the Lord said to Gideon, 'All those who lap the water with their tongues, as a dog laps, you shall put to one side; all those who kneel down to drink, putting their hands to their mouths, you shall put to the other side.' The number of those that lapped was three hundred; but all the rest of the troops knelt down to drink water. Then the Lord said to Gideon, 'With the three hundred that lapped I will deliver you, and give the Midianites into your hand. Let all the others go to their homes.' So he took the jars of the troops from their hands, and their trumpets; and he sent all the rest of Israel back to their own tents, but retained the three hundred. The camp of Midian was below him in the valley.

In the previous reading, as we looked at the story of Gideon, we were thinking about how God can take us as we are, even if we feel small and afraid, and make us ready to do the task which he has set before us. As we read on, we see that God does not ask Gideon merely to lead his people to victory. He expects him to do it against all the odds, that is, with very few helpers.

You can imagine that Gideon was feeling rather pleased with himself. The timid coward of the beginning of chapter 6 has been transformed into the general of an army of 32,000 troops by the beginning of chapter 7. Not bad going, you might think.

But God has different ideas. Gradually, but firmly, he cuts down the size of Gideon's army, until only three hundred men are left. Humanly speaking, Gideon was left with very few resources at all.

Being a new parent can make us feel like Gideon. You may have given up work to care for your new baby, or you may have taken maternity or paternity leave, but as we leave the security and predictability of a work environment, even if it is just for a few months, it can feel as if we have lost part of our identity. However much we like or dislike our employment, it gives a structure and often a network of contacts and friends whom we inevitably miss when we are not there. Colleagues may also regard us rather differently as new parents, and assume that we no longer want to go out or talk about anything but the best disposable nappies and cures for cradle-cap. So we also lose our social network, which for most of us is an important resource for coping with everyday life.

It may not just be our social life that we find is compromised. Time alone with God, or even time spent with other Christians, is also affected. Daily devotional times have to be grabbed while the baby sleeps or feeds, and are regularly disturbed by other demands. When we do have a few undisturbed minutes, it can be hard to concentrate, when our bodies want most of all to rest. For most of us, the pattern of our devotional life will need rethinking. Bible reading notes can help, but even praying when it is a struggle to stay awake can be very frustrating. Trying to maintain our previous pattern may leave us with a sense of failure before God.

Joining in the corporate worship of the church with a new baby can be hard. A sleeping baby can wake at any time, and it is virtually impossible not to be distracted in your worship by a baby's presence. Whenever I tried it, I was always painfully aware of the distraction that was caused to others sitting around us. Most people do not seem to mind a baby in church, but when you are aware that your child is distracting a number of people and preventing them from fully participating in the service, it can feel awkward. Remember, though, that you and your child are a vitally important part of your church congregation, and you should be welcomed and supported by other members of it. A new baby in any congregation should remind people of the creative power of God, and is something to get excited about.

So, by the time our employment, our social life, our devotional life, and our church involvement have been disrupted, we may feel, like Gideon, that all our layers of support have been stripped away. Our relationships with others may have to be adapted, and in some cases abandoned. Our relationship with God may also feel different, particularly if we are people who have previously been at all kinds of church meetings and events. Now may be the time to realize and rely on the fact that God loves you for who you are, *not* for what you do for him! And all this comes at a time when you are physically drained and exhausted. Being a new parent can be very hard, and you end up feeling vulnerable and unable to cope.

But do not lose heart. Gideon lacked confidence, even though he was following God's directions to him. If we go on reading Judges 7, it tells how God acknowledged that Gideon was feeling nervous and exposed, and allowed him to hear what the enemy was saying. When all our old resources and coping methods have gone, and we feel unable to face the new challenges before us, we still have a God who understands and will carry us through our uncertainty.

Gideon went on to divide his small army of men into three groups of one hundred. Then, armed simply with trumpets, jars and torches, they went off in the night to face their enemy. The noise of their shouts of the Lord's victory, trumpets and smashing of jars, and the sudden light from the previously hidden torches, were enough to throw their enemies into panic and confusion, so that they turned on each other and fled. God led Gideon and his people into victory over their seemingly stronger and more powerful enemy because Gideon was prepared to obey God's commands to him. He was willing to trust God as all of his resources were taken away, until all he was left with was God. Gideon faced the challenge that God gave him, and he ended up stronger, wiser and much more able to cope with his situation. He is even listed in Hebrews 11 along with other Old Testament characters who had incredible faith in God.

I hope that looking briefly at the story of Gideon has encouraged you as you face some of the challenges that being a new parent poses.

If you feel that all you used to depend on has been taken away, then turn to the God of Gideon, who had to strip away all the human resources that Gideon could find, so that he learnt to trust in God who gave him the victory.

**Prayer**

*God of Gideon, who taught him faith and trust when he was small and weak, and who brought him to the point of victory, meet with us in a similar way, at this time when our resources have been stripped away. Help us to be as faithful and reliant on you as Gideon was. Amen*

# 'Without counsel, plans go wrong; with many advisers they succeed'

**Luke 1:57–66 (NRSV)**

Now the time came for Elizabeth to give birth, and she bore a son. Her neighbours and relatives heard that the Lord had shown his great mercy to her, and they rejoiced with her.

On the eighth day they came to circumcise the child, and they were going to name him Zechariah after his father. But his mother said, 'No; he is to be called John.' They said to her, 'None of your relatives has this name.' Then they began motioning to his father to find out what name he wanted to give him. He asked for a writing tablet and wrote, 'His name is John.' And all of them were amazed. Immediately his mouth was opened and his tongue freed, and he began to speak, praising God. Fear came over all their neighbours, and all these things were talked about throughout the entire hill country of Judea. All who heard them pondered them and said, 'What then will this child become?' For, indeed, the hand of the Lord was with him.

There is nothing like the birth of a child to bring people out of the woodwork. No sooner has the joyful news gone out via the phone lines or the garish birth announcement cards, than the friends and relations begin to gather. Our Bible reading tells us that things were no different in first-century Judea. Elizabeth's neighbours and relatives rejoiced with her, we read. No doubt they congregated at the house, queuing for their chance to kiss the baby, leaving trails of knitted baby bootees (or their first-century equivalent) all over the place. Many of us have had a similar experience. Depending on how we are feeling at the time, this may or may not be a good thing.

What is rarely a good thing is the advice that our friends and families bring with them. There is nothing wrong with advice in itself. The title chosen for today is a quote from Proverbs that reminds us of the value of advice. Often, others have insights or experiences which help us in situations we face, and we are foolish to ignore them. Others who have travelled the same road before us may be able to help us to complete our journey successfully. But the problem with having a child is that everybody seems to have some advice to offer, and much of it is contradictory. Everyone who has had a child considers himself or herself an expert when their friends and loved ones have children too.

So almost every visitor brings with them another golden nugget of wisdom which they found invaluable when their children were born. It may be to do with breast-feeding or bottle-feeding, or where the baby should sleep and in what position, or how to respond when the baby cries. Often, these opinions can be urged upon us quite forcefully, particularly by our parents who may want us to do things the way they did them. Sometimes our well-meaning relations can appear quite hurt when it becomes obvious to them that we do not intend to do things in the same way.

What can be more worrying is when medical advice from midwives, nurses and doctors is similarly contradictory. Friends of ours initially faced a worrying time after the birth of their first child, when the baby, who had been small at birth, failed to put on weight. They searched in vain for a consensus amongst the medical professionals about what was wrong, how serious it was, and what should be done about it. At a time that was already highly stressful, they had to deal with the added pressure of not knowing who to believe or what advice to take.

In the case of John the Baptist, the beginning of whose story we read today, there was a specific issue on which the visiting friends and relatives were united. The issue was the baby's name.

Surely no subject that arises around the birth of a baby has more capacity to rouse strong feelings than this one. Couples who pride themselves on agreeing about virtually everything can end up in violent disagreement over it. Parents who have consciously kept their opinions to themselves over many years can no longer be restrained. Expectant mums-to-be who forget everything they hear at antenatal classes as soon as the class is over lie awake at night silently turning over the possibilities. Fashion, taste and family tradition combine in a potentially explosive cocktail when it comes to choosing a name for the baby.

Before our first child was born, we made the mistake of telling Stephen's mother what names we had chosen: Natalie for a girl, Jacob for a boy. When we had a daughter, the new grandmother almost clapped her hands with joy. 'I'm so glad it wasn't a boy,' she beamed. 'I don't think I could have stood to see you name him Jacob!' We still think Jacob is a rather good name, in fact, but it has been ruled out of consideration for successive children because of this exchange.

At least Zechariah and Elizabeth didn't have to debate the choice of name themselves. Ever since the angel Gabriel appeared to Zechariah and told him of the child's conception, there was no chance of any other choice but John. The neighbours didn't like it, but they were just going to have to put up with it.

And when all is said and done, we have to have the same attitude. Advice can be helpful, but it is we who are parents who ultimately have to make decisions. Advice is like a very rich chocolate pudding. A little of it can go a long way. Often, different people's advice is contradictory anyway, so even if we wanted to we could not take all of it. The fact is that God has entrusted responsibility for each new life to its parents, and it is they who have to do what they believe to be best. Whether it is choosing names, establishing a sleep pattern, feeding, or anything else, we can listen to good advice when it is offered, but we need also to listen to our own instincts and to the voice of the Spirit within us, and then make the choice we believe to be right.

**Prayer**

*Dear God, thank you for the people you have placed in our lives who care enough to offer advice. Please give to us sufficient confidence in our own judgment and instincts, and sensitivity to your guidance, that we may be able to accept advice when it is helpful and cheerfully disregard it when it isn't. Amen*

# A time for everything

**Ecclesiastes 3:1–8 (NRSV)**

For everything there is a season,
and a time for every matter under heaven:
a time to be born, and a time to die;
a time to plant, and a time to pluck up what is planted;
a time to kill, and a time to heal;
a time to break down, and a time to build up;
a time to weep, and a time to laugh;
a time to mourn, and a time to dance;
a time to throw away stones, and a time to gather stones together;
a time to embrace, and a time to refrain from embracing;
a time to seek, and a time to lose;
a time to keep, and a time to throw away;
a time to tear, and a time to sew;
a time to keep silence, and a time to speak;
a time to love, and a time to hate;
a time for war, and a time for peace.

Time for everything? That's not how it feels. *Never* time for *anything* might be more accurate. Not enough time for sleep. Not enough time for conversation. Not enough time to have a meal without interruption. Not enough time to watch a film on the television or listen to a piece of music. Not enough time for friends. Not enough time to clean or tidy. Not even enough time for the baby, not to do all the things we wanted to do when children came along.

You don't have to be a parent to feel like this, apart from the bit about the baby, obviously. More and more people feel like this all day every day. There never seems to be enough time to do everything that we want to do, or even need to do. Years ago, we were told how the technological revolution was going to give us almost limitless time. The main challenge of the late twentieth century would be how to fill it. No one would work more than two or three days a week, gadgets and gizmos would do the dull domestic jobs, and we would be people of leisure. Nobody has talked like this for many years now. In fact, we seem to have less time than ever. The pressures of our hi-tech age seem to be greater, not less, than those of earlier, simpler times. We do more things more quickly than any generation before us, and the wonderful technology seems to exist just to force us to attempt still more.

So there are probably some parents reading this book who in years gone by would be at home caring for the new baby full-time. Instead they are managing to go on working from home, by the miracles of video conferencing, e-mail, and the Internet. There are other parents who, on returning home from the office, might have expected to be finished for the day, but now bring work home on their laptop computer, so as to be able to fulfil the unrealistic expectations of their employer.

How, then, do we cope when, on top of all the demands placed upon our time in an increasingly time-famished world, a baby comes along who has no regard for our schedules, no concern about the early morning meeting for which we have to be prepared, no idea of the value of each precious minute in our packed day?

Part of the answer is found in this passage from Ecclesiastes 3. We read that there is a time to be born. We might also say that there is a time to give birth, and a time to devote ourselves to children.

It should be common sense that the time when we are adjusting to parenting is not the best time to take on other things in our lives. It isn't the ideal time to seek promotion, or move house, or begin a course of study, or take on some new ministry. Of course, our lives aren't ideal a lot of the time, and we may have good reasons for feeling that we have to do one of those things at just this moment. But it probably isn't the best time.

Having a child, joyful experience though it generally is, is also one of the most stressful things we ever do. It takes our time, our energy, our concentration. If we tackle another demanding challenge at the same time, we can find ourselves exhausted, run down, stressed out.

This means that we have to learn to go easy on ourselves. The daily standards we set for ourselves—and attained—before the baby was born may not be realistic any more. Stephen remembers going to a conference with the staff team of the church where he was ministering soon after one of our children was born, and feeling very frustrated with himself because, although it was evidently a very good conference, he couldn't get anything out of it. He wasn't able to concentrate on the speakers, or participate fully in the worship. Finally, a colleague said, 'Of course you aren't getting as much out of this as you would like. You haven't had an undisturbed night's sleep for months. You're tired and preoccupied.' She was right. It wasn't that he had lost interest in the subject of the conference, or lost his ability to listen and learn. But this wasn't the time for conferences. It was the time for adjusting to parenthood.

Few of us have the luxury of deciding that we will make this our parenting time, with no other pressures and distractions. Money still has to be earnt, bills still have to be paid, food still has to be bought and cooked. But if we can recognize that the focus of this next year or two will be different from the focus of the last year or two, it may free us to enjoy this time without setting ourselves too many other things to do. After all, each child's life has seasons as well. The first smile, the first words, the magical process of exploring and developing—these moments won't come back again. We need to appreciate this time for the precious thing that it is, and leave, as far as we are able, other goals and activities for their appropriate season.

**Prayer**

*Heavenly Father, thank you for the gift of this time, with its joys and challenges, its tears and laughter. Please help us to appreciate this time for the precious thing that it is, and so to make the best of every moment. Amen.*

# Strength for the weary

**Isaiah 40:25–31 (NIV)**

'To whom will you compare me?
Or who is my equal?' says the Holy One.
Lift your eyes and look to the heavens:
Who created all these?
He who brings out the starry host one by one,
and calls them each by name.
Because of his great power and mighty strength,
not one of them is missing.
Why do you say, O Jacob,
and complain, O Israel,
'My way is hidden from the Lord;
my cause is disregarded by my God'?
Do you not know?
Have you not heard?
The Lord is the everlasting God,
the Creator of the ends of the earth.
He will not grow tired or weary,
and his understanding no one can fathom.
He gives strength to the weary
and increases the power of the weak.
Even youths grow tired and weary,
and young men stumble and fall;
but those who hope in the Lord
will renew their strength.
They will soar on wings like eagles;
they will run and not grow weary,
they will walk and not be faint.

As the father of young children, with a demanding job and other commitments too, I sometimes allow myself to become over-tired. In fact, I have struggled with this since I was a teenager.

When I was nineteen or twenty years old, I was in danger of wearing myself out. I had left school with disappointing A' Level results and was working in a bank. Before I went to work every morning, I would spend one to two hours on academic work preparing to retake my A' Levels. In the evenings I was preoccupied with my church youth group, of which I was a leader. Often, I would be talking and praying with people until past midnight, before getting up at 5.30 or 6 a.m. to begin my studies again. By the time I had been living like this for a few months, I was exhausted. I wondered where I was going to find the strength for another day.

All in all, it was good preparation for parenting. The endless hours, the short or broken nights, the pressures of juggling two or three demanding things at once, are things that are all too familiar to parents of young children.

Just when I thought I was coming to the end of my resources, someone gave me a Christmas card (it was Christmas time!) with the reference Isaiah 40:25–31 written inside. I read this passage perhaps for the first time and through it God spoke to me. In fact, he did more than speak to me. I felt him touch me and renew me and give me strength.

There have been many times since then when I have felt worn out, stressed out, or burnt out. For example, the summer when our oldest child was born was also the summer that I left theological college and was ordained. We moved house with a six-week-old baby, and plunged into the business of a lively, thriving parish. The baby didn't sleep, and the work didn't wait. Quite soon I was running on empty, at least as far as my human reserves were concerned. Even today as I write this, I am feeling the after-effects of another disturbed night, not because of the children this time, but other pressures and anxieties. The end of my 'To Do' list seems a long way away, and energy is flagging.

Many other parents experience something similar. Whether it is trying to juggle work around a demanding baby, or seeking to care properly for older children as well as a newborn infant, or simply trying to maintain the balance of an ordered life in the face of the disruption brought by a new child, we quite quickly become worn down and worn out. This may catch us by surprise. Those of us who are younger, say in our 20s and 30s, may be used to feeling energetic, lively, able to cope. But Isaiah reminds us that even the young grow tired and weary, and many of us know from our own experience that this is true.

Where do we turn when we feel like this? This passage from Isaiah points us back to the One who is the source of all our energy, all our strength, all our life. He alone will not grow tired or weary. He alone has such boundless vigour that he is able to give strength to the weary and power to the weak. So Isaiah tells us that those who turn to God even in their weakness will find their strength renewed.

The picture here is not of mere survival. Isaiah gives us three images of the renewed strength of the person who is hoping in the Lord. This person will walk and not be faint. Walking is the most ordinary, the most mundane way we have of getting from A to B. Isaiah says we will be able to keep going with the ordinary, the mundane, the everyday, without being ground down by it. Secondly, this person will run and not grow weary. Running involves a burst of energy, and is something we can do only for a while. Yet Isaiah says that we will be able to sustain that burst of energy without becoming weary. Thirdly, this person will fly like an eagle. If you watch how an eagle flies, you see how easy it looks. The eagle does not flap frantically, desperately trying to stay in the air. Rather, he trusts in the air currents themselves to carry him along.

We need to learn how to be like an eagle, not wearing ourselves out with constant flapping, but learning to glide on the air currents, the winds of the Holy Spirit. That isn't easy. Sometimes we feel we lack the skills to discern where those currents are. Sometimes the winds of the Spirit may not be going in the direction we wanted to go. Most of us naturally rely on our own ability to flap harder to keep us up in the air. But that way leads to exhaustion, frustration and disappointment. I don't think I have learned yet how to ride on the winds of the Spirit, to let myself be carried by One more powerful than I. But I am committed to learning, because I am sure that it is only as I do, that the promise of God's power in my weakness becomes a reality in my life.

**Prayer**

*Almighty God, you promise strength for the weary and rest for the heavy-laden. Please help us to learn to ride on the winds of the Spirit, and to be carried along by him, so that we may be sustained by your great power. Amen*

# Under pressure

**Jeremiah 17:5–10 (NRSV)**

Thus says the Lord:
Cursed are those who trust in mere mortals
    and make mere flesh their strength,
    whose hearts turn away from the Lord.
They shall be like a shrub in the desert,
    and shall not see when relief comes.
They shall live in the parched places of the wilderness,
    in an uninhabited salt land.
Blessed are those who trust in the Lord,
    whose trust is the Lord.
They shall be like a tree planted by water,
    sending out its roots by the stream.
It shall not fear when heat comes,
    and its leaves shall stay green;
in the year of drought it is not anxious,
    and it does not cease to bear fruit.
The heart is devious above all else;
    it is perverse—
    who can understand it?
I the Lord test the mind
    and search the heart,
to give to all according to their ways,
    according to the fruit of their doings.

When we are under pressure, the *real* person shows through.

On the cross, Jesus said, 'Father, forgive them, for they do not know what they are doing' (Luke 23:34). When he had been beaten and abandoned and was dying, Christ demonstrated his character as it truly was. None of us is ever likely to face the kind of testing that Jesus faced, and none of us could honestly say that if we did face such a test,

we would respond in such a way. But all of us face pressure at certai
times in our lives, and when we do, our true nature comes through.

Throughout the Bible, and in the Old Testament in particula people are regularly divided into two groups: those who trust in Go and those who do not; those who fear the Lord and those who do not those who walk in the light and those who walk in darkness. In th New Testament, Jesus talks about how the sheep and the goats will b divided on the last day. Jeremiah uses this type of distinction in ou passage for today. On one hand there are those who trust i humankind for their strength, and on the other hand there are thos who trust in God. Jeremiah describes how the person who trusts i their own strength and relies on other people will not see God' blessing. Then he goes on to say that someone who trusts in God an has their inner core firmly established in God will know God' presence. It is a common biblical theme, and as Christians we mos naturally identify ourselves with those who trust God, who walk in th light of his word.

When Jeremiah goes on to speak about the deceitfulness of th human heart, we may quickly read past it, assuming that he is referrin here to those who do not acknowledge God. The structure of th passage suggests otherwise. After describing both types of peopl Jeremiah says, 'The heart is devious above all else; it is perverse—wh can understand it?' (v. 9).

By implication, this applies as much to those who look to Go for their strength as those who look to other things. All of us, God worshipper or not, have hearts which are fundamentally flawed, whos depths are unfathomable, says Jeremiah.

Not all of us can admit that this is true. But at times when we ar under stress and pressure we may get a glimpse of what Jeremiah i talking about. The real me is seen most clearly when I am unde pressure.

As a child and a young adult, Stephen had a quick temper. As h grew older, he lost his temper less and less frequently, so he felt that h was growing out of this characteristic. But subsequently, when he wa working too hard or sleeping badly, he would find that bad tempe returning. What was happening? Jeremiah would say that what was i the heart all along was being revealed under pressure. It is dispiriting t discover that we have not so much grown out of a particular personality flaw as we have learned to control it more effectively.

In the aftermath of having a baby, we can find ourselves in that position. The strain on our relationship with our partner, the lack of social support and the overwhelming tiredness begin to take their toll. When we reach this point, it can be quite horrifying to hear what comes out of our mouths, or see the behaviour patterns that we display. I cannot remember how many guilt-ridden new parents I have heard describing how they left their screaming child in a cot, slammed the door, and had to get right away, or something similar. Others have found that things about their spouse which have niggled for years now become the stuff of shouting matches and threatened divorces. It is not that the other partner has changed, nor that the child is particularly naughty. Rather, under pressure, everything that is bubbling away under the surface bursts through.

In Matthew's Gospel, when Jesus is speaking to the Pharisees, he says, 'Out of the overflow of the heart the mouth speaks' (Matthew 12:34, NIV). What we are in our hearts is going to come out in what we say and how we behave, especially when we are under pressure. It can be very difficult for us to deal with the fact that these feelings and emotions are inside us at all. It can be even more difficult to accept that they may erupt out of us, even publicly at times. The easiest escape routes are denial, pretending that this isn't happening, or transference, pretending that it is only another person—perhaps our marriage partner—who has the problem. But the things we express in our words and behaviour are part of our human nature, and it is only by acknowledging them that we can begin to deal with them.

We may find that in this time of new stresses and challenges, we have to face up to aspects of ourselves that we had kept hidden deep within for a long time. In many ways this can be the most difficult challenge of all for us as new parents, as we find out more about ourselves than we wanted to, or wanted other people to. Even worse, we are probably experiencing this alongside a husband or wife who is going through something similar.

The key to the whole process is being realistic about the kinds of people that we are, our strengths and our well-camouflaged weaknesses, so that we can be realistic about ourselves and each other. As we do this, God can work to bring healing and freedom, to make us more and more the people he had always intended that we should be.

**Prayer**

*Lord God, I know that deep within me are all sorts of thoughts, feelings and characteristics which I would rather pretend were not there. When I am tired or under pressure, some of these things come out. They shock me and perhaps others too. Please help me to be honest with you and those closest to me about what is really in my heart. That way, I will grow in my relationships with them and with you, and you can begin your healing work in me. Amen*

# The oil of grace

**Ezekiel 47:1, 3–5, 7–9 (NRSV)**

Then he brought me back to the entrance of the temple; there, water was flowing from below the threshold of the temple toward the east (for the temple faced east); and the water was flowing down from below the south end of the threshold of the temple, south of the altar...

Going on eastward with a cord in his hand, the man measured one thousand cubits, and then led me through the water; and it was ankle-deep.

Again he measured one thousand, and led me through the water; and it was knee-deep. Again he measured one thousand, and led me through the water; and it was up to the waist.

Again he measured one thousand, and it was a river that I could not cross, for the water had risen; it was deep enough to swim in, a river that could not be crossed...

As I came back, I saw on the bank of the river a great many trees on the one side and on the other. He said to me, 'This water flows toward the eastern region and goes down into the Arabah; and when it enters the sea, the sea of stagnant waters, the water will become fresh. Wherever the river goes, every living creature that swarms will live, and there will be very many fish, once these waters reach there. It will become fresh; and everything will live where the river goes.'

A recent family holiday started badly. We had been driving for an hour or so, from the bustle and fumes of London to the hoped-for peace of Cornwall, when the engine began to make clattering noises that even I—a non-mechanic—recognized as heralding bad news. As I moved the car across into the inside lane, the clanging and crunching grew louder until, with a final ominous bang, the engine stopped. We came to a standstill on the hard shoulder. The children began to cry.

Even the briefest examination of the car and its environment made clear that something was seriously wrong. Lifting the bonnet revealed an engine spattered with oil. The tarmac beneath the car was rapidly disappearing beneath a shiny black puddle. The stretch of road we had been driving on was smeared with traces of oil too.

Whatever else might have been wrong with the car—and we soon found out that a lot was wrong—the fact that all that oil which should have been in the engine, smoothing its operation and enabling it to run efficiently, was now liberally distributed along the M4 meant that we weren't going to Cornwall that day. By bedtime we were back home again, organizing a hire car so we could try again the next morning.

Stephen's mum says that when she was first a parent caring for two young children, she made a point of saying a prayer every morning, that God would give her grace for the day ahead. If she forgot to say that prayer, as the hours ticked by she would feel that something was missing, until she remembered, and stopped, and prayed. As she prayed, she would picture the grace of God as oil, not dirty black motor oil, but fresh golden oil, pouring over her and her children and her day. Just as the car needed the flow of oil to ensure its smooth running, so she needed the soothing oil of grace to help her survive another day with young children.

To be a Christian is to be someone who has begun to taste the grace of God—his love and acceptance of us, the abundance of his joy in us, the resources of his mercy and peace made available to us. We may feel that our experience of this grace is strictly limited, and yet it has been said that it is the emphasis on the grace of God that makes Christianity unique as a world religion. Every Christian knows something of the oil of grace.

Ezekiel 47 is a Bible passage which has been much quoted in some churches in recent years, often in the context of talking about the renewing work of the Holy Spirit. But whatever else it may be about, it is a picture of the grace of God. The image here is not of the steady trickle of pouring oil, but of the accelerating rush of water, as a tiny stream turns into a mighty river, and is finally swallowed up by the sea. Yet these pictures, of the river and the oil, have similarities. They are both pictures of richness on one hand, and real essentials on the other. Oil in the ancient Near East was a basic staple of everyday life, and yet could be a real extravagance, as in the story of the anointing of Jesus' feet by Mary. The water of the river is necessary for mere survival, and yet is pictured here in unstinting abundance. It's a river that begins in the temple, symbolizing God himself. At its beginning, it is small enough to paddle in, to splash and play beside. At its end, it is awesome and overpowering, uncontrollable, and yet the source of all sorts of life.

Our experience of God's grace may be like that. Wherever we have got to in our spiritual journey, there is always more to discover and experience. We may be tempted sometimes to think that we have the measure of God's grace, yet those who have most experience of it know that it is immeasurable. God's grace is inexhaustible. It never comes to an end. The more of it we receive, the more we know there is for us still to receive.

And it is when we reach the limit of our finite resources and capabilities that we need it most. It is when we're tired, fed up, disappointed, disillusioned, that we most need to turn to God and ask for his grace for this day. When we've been up since before dawn with a sleepless child, and we're wondering how we're going to get through the day; when our social life has collapsed, and we want nothing more than to be in bed before 10pm; when a nappy needs changing yet again just as we're leaving the house for an appointment for which we were already late, we need God's grace. And it is as we ask that we receive.

As we waited by our expensively ruined car at the side of the M4 for someone to come and tow us home, I knew I needed another kind of oil just as much as our spilt engine oil. I needed the oil of grace.

**Prayer**

*Dear Father God, we thank you for your gift of grace, made available to us each day, if we only ask. Please pour out upon me and into me the oil of grace, that I might face each situation with your resources, knowing that you are never more than a prayer away. I ask this in Jesus' name. Amen*

# Forgiving and forgiven

**Matthew 18:21–28, 32–33 (NRSV)**

Peter came and said to [Jesus], 'Lord, if another member of the church sins against me, how often should I forgive? As many as seven times?' Jesus said to him, 'Not seven times, but, I tell you, seventy-seven times.

'For this reason the kingdom of heaven may be compared to a king who wished to settle accounts with his slaves. When he began the reckoning, one who owed him ten thousand talents was brought to him; and, as he could not pay, his lord ordered him to be sold, together with his wife and children and all his possessions, and payment to be made. So the slave fell on his knees before him, saying, "Have patience with me, and I will pay you everything." And out of pity for him, the lord of that slave released him and forgave him the debt. But that same slave, as he went out, came upon one of his fellow slaves who owed him a hundred denarii; and seizing him by the throat, he said, "Pay what you owe." …

'Then his lord summoned him and said to him, "You wicked slave! I forgave you all that debt because you pleaded with me. Should you not have had mercy on your fellow slave, as I had mercy on you?"'

Jesus understood a lot more about teaching than most of the preachers and speakers we have in the church today. While preachers' sermons are often filled with instructions and exhortations, Jesus knew that our spiritual lives are often more profoundly formed by the prayers we pray and the stories that furnish our imagination. So to teach us about forgiveness, he gave us a prayer ('Forgive us our sins as we forgive those who sin against us') and a story.

Peter, rather like a precocious child in a Sunday school class, asks a question which he hopes will demonstrate his own great understanding of Jesus and his teaching. The rabbis of the day taught that someone who had been wronged should forgive three times. Peter suggests that he should forgive seven times, no doubt expecting to be complimented on his generosity. Jesus' response is really a way of saying that there should be no limit on our forgiveness. In his parable he explains why this is so.

A king is owed ten thousand talents by a slave. This is an unimaginable amount of money. King Herod's annual income was only nine hundred talents. It is inconceivable that a slave could owe a king that kind of sum. Jesus is really saying, 'Imagine a debt from which there is no way out, a debt so vast that there could be no chance of ever repaying it, so that the debtor would be dependent on the mercy of the other person every day of his life.' It is this debt, millions of pounds in today's money, that the king writes off.

In our debt-ridden culture, many people know what it is to accumulate debts that seem insurmountable. Some end up borrowing to pay back the earlier loans, until there is no more money to move around, and catastrophe lies ahead. That is how the man in the story must have felt. And then, unexpectedly, miraculously, the king says, 'There is no way you are ever going to be able to pay this off. We'll forget all about it.' It's as if the bank manager were to call me in to his office to tell me that he had added up my mortgage, car loan, personal loan, credit card bill and overdraft, and he doubted my ability ever to pay it all back, so he had decided to cancel the lot. I would come out skipping and singing and dancing down the street, and that is the reaction we expect from the man in the story.

But, of course, that is not the case. Instead of exulting in his newfound freedom, this man sets off to pursue a debt so tiny it would hardly seem worth collecting. The first sum is the gross domestic product of a small country. The second is the month's paper bill. So hard-hearted is the villain of the piece that the overwhelming mercy of the king has moved him not at all. His fellow slaves are stunned that their forgiven colleague behaves in this way, and report him to the king, who then deals with him with the same degree of mercy that he himself has shown.

In our families, we too need to learn about forgiveness. Anyone who has had relationships of any depth at all must have experienced the joyful freedom of forgiveness given and received, and perhaps the corrosive coldness of forgiveness withheld. Many marriages are stunted and withered by an attitude that still recalls wrongs, real and imagined, from episodes long past.

Under new pressures of sleepless nights, professional status relinquished and new roles evolving, submerged hurts from the past can all too easily be dredged up again. At the same time, new bones of contention can emerge which, if unresolved, hold the seeds of the bitterness of the future. Arguments about who gets up to the crying baby at night, why the house isn't as tidy as it used to be, what vestiges of a social life can and can't be maintained, are perfectly healthy if addressed and worked through. Ignored and buried, they may fester away inside us, waiting to explode at some moment in the future. As marriage partners, and new parents, we need to learn how to ask for, give and receive forgiveness. That doesn't mean pretending that no wrong has been done, but rather acknowledging hurt caused deliberately and unwittingly, and consciously letting go of it.

All of this is also necessary in our relationships with our children, however young they may be. 'Forgive a young child?' someone might ask. 'What could they need forgiving for?'

Forgiveness is not just about wrong objectively done, but about our responses to things which might not be the other person's fault at all. One child was conceived to replace a brother who had died, and was resented by his parents for taking the place of their dead child. Other parents have borne grudges against their children for being the 'wrong' sex, or taking after the 'wrong' side of the family, or reflecting the characteristics which they disliked in themselves. Forgiveness is the process by which we acknowledge those feelings in us, and release them.

But harder still is learning to ask our own children to forgive us when we have done wrong. When we lose our temper with a child unjustifiably, it is easier to excuse and explain why I have done it than it is to say sorry and to ask forgiveness, yet that is what is needed. When we are prepared to admit our mistakes to our children, to let them see that even Daddy or Mummy sometimes gets it wrong, somehow it brings us closer together. Parents and children alike need forgiveness, from God and from each other.

Many of us, when our children are born, have a mental image of the perfect family life which we hope to enjoy. We're not going to make the mistakes our parents made, we vow. We've read the books, listened to our friends, watched the TV programmes to help us succeed as parents. Yet when we get started, we discover that we are still the same frail people, with all the same faults and hang-ups that we had before. What's worse is that we soon discover that the new additions to our family are far from perfect too. Forgiveness is the way we deal with the gap between the ideal and the reality.

Jesus in his parable reminds us that to give forgiveness we need to have experienced it. The forgiven servant should have been able to forgive because he himself had been forgiven. If we know ourselves, and are honest with ourselves, we know that we have sinned against God far more that anyone has ever sinned against us, and yet he has forgiven and goes on forgiving 'seventy times seven'—forgiveness without limit. As we experience the wonder of being forgiven by God, so we are able to forgive wrongs real and imagined, and so know the joy that the slave in the parable so tragically missed.

**Prayer**

*Father in heaven, thank you that through Jesus you have forgiven us freely, totally, of our debts against you. Please fill us with the joy that forgiveness brings, and so enable us to seek forgiveness for the wrongs we do to others and to offer forgiveness when we are wronged. Amen*

# Adopted as children

**Galatians 3:26—4:7 (NRSV)**

In Christ Jesus you are all children of God through faith. As many of you as were baptized into Christ have clothed yourselves with Christ. There is no longer Jew or Greek, there is no longer slave or free, there is no longer male and female; for all of you are one in Christ Jesus. And if you belong to Christ, then you are Abraham's offspring, heirs according to the promise. My point is this: heirs, as long as they are minors, are no better than slaves, though they are the owners of all the property; but they remain under guardians and trustees until the date set by the father. So with us; while we were minors, we were enslaved to the elemental spirits of the world. But when the fullness of time had come, God sent his Son, born of a woman, born under the law, in order to redeem those who were under the law, so that we might receive adoption as children. And because you are children, God has sent the Spirit of his Son into our hearts, crying, 'Abba! Father!' So you are no longer a slave but a child, and if a child then also an heir, through God.

In 'New Responsibilities 5', we referred to the stories which families pass down about earlier generations. Very recently we have heard some of those stories ourselves.

At the beginning of the week that we wrote this, Jacqui's grandma died. As she was rushed into hospital, dangerously ill, relatives began to arrive from far-flung corners of the country. Because our home was the nearest to her home, they based themselves with us.

As it became clear that Grandma wasn't going to survive the weekend, there were tearful farewell visits, and difficult decisions about what medical treatment should or shouldn't be accepted. Life support machines were switched off, and the waiting began.

Meanwhile, members of the family swapped stories and recollections, sometimes poignantly, other times with real laughter. We heard again about the annual Windsor Conservatives Garden Party where Jacqui helped as a little girl, about last year's bonfire party when Grandma danced with our four-year-old daughter to some cheesy hit from the 1970s. For those who had known her all their lives—children, grandchildren, great-grandchildren—these stories were part of their heritage, their identity. These stories have helped to make our family what it is, to make individual family members what they are.

All of us are shaped to some extent by the stories we have been born into, the relationships we have experienced, for better or worse. Some are fortunate. A close and caring family gives a sense of security as they grow up. There is a feeling of belonging, of being accepted and wanted, of being part of the bigger story of their family, not just an isolated individual. Others are not so lucky. They are born into a family that is coming apart at the seams, perhaps one where there is cruelty or violence or abuse. They may grow up wondering where they belong, who wants them.

Computer buffs have an expression: garbage in, garbage out. Sadly, what is true for computers is also true for people. When we first have children of our own, this becomes sharply relevant to our own situation. All the evidence is that those of us who have grown up knowing we are wanted and cared for, secure in who we are, find it easier to offer our own children that same environment. Conversely, those of us who have suffered neglect, fear or abusive relationships in childhood may find ourselves reproducing the same hardships on our own children. In this sense, the sins of the fathers may truly be visited on their children.

We need the security of knowing that we belong in a bigger story, knowing we are cherished and wanted, knowing that those who care for us think the best of us, so that we can pass on the same sense of security and identity to our children. In this way, security and self-confidence are passed on from generation to generation.

Jesus was the example *par excellence* of this. He, alone in history, was the perfectly secure man. He knew who he was and what his life's mission was, and he would not be deflected from it by anyone else's agenda. He alone never responded to situations out of pique or bitterness or wounded pride. He was able to cope with other people's opposition, even hatred, because of that quiet confidence which characterized everything he did. The key to this strong sense of identity was that Jesus knew who he was in relation to his Father. Whatever affirmation he may or may not have received from his human parents, Jesus was affirmed by his heavenly Father: 'This is my beloved Son, with whom I am well pleased.' Jesus also knew who he was in relation to a bigger story of which he was the centre, the story of God's redemptive activity in the world. This was a story which stretched back through David, Moses and Abraham, and would stretch forward into the future too.

But then, what hope is there for the rest of us? Are we condemned endlessly to repeat the mistakes our parents made, passing all our little hang-ups and inadequacies on to our children?

Paul, writing to the Galatians, would say not. Whatever our life experience to date, however confident and secure or broken and vulnerable it may have left us, there is hope for change, because the same Spirit who came upon Jesus when he was affirmed by his Father at his baptism has also been poured out upon all who have been baptized in his name. Through that work of the Spirit, we have been adopted as children of God. Our story has been joined to his.

Roman law made no distinctions between an adopted child and a biological one. Their status and rights of inheritance were identical. So it is with us, who have been adopted as God's children. That's why we can address God by the same ordinary everyday word for Dad—'abba'—that Jesus used. We, as Christians, have come into the same kind of relationship of closeness and intimacy with God that Jesus enjoyed. As we explore and develop that relationship, so we can begin to experience for ourselves the perfect acceptance and affirmation from the Father that Jesus knew.

Not only that, but in our adoption into God's family we become part of the same big story that Jesus knew he was part of. Our Bible passage makes that clear: 'If you belong to Christ, then you are Abraham's offspring' (Galatians 3:29). Just as we, when we marry, became part of the story of our spouse's family, so we have become part of the story of God's people, of God's action in the world.

So we don't have to endlessly relive the brokenness of our relationships and life experience so far. Instead, we can make God's story our story, so that we know who we are. We can take his affirmation of us as his children, chosen and adopted, to heart, so that we become secure in our relationship with him. We can ask him to pour his loving, healing Spirit into our hearts, so that things which have been broken in the past can be made whole again. And we can determine to live as parents out of our growing experience of his love, his light, his grace, so that in time our children come to know that they are his children too.

Of course, we still won't be perfect parents. None of us is. We will still make mistakes, and slip back into patterns we thought we had left behind. But as we know ourselves to be passionately, unconditionally, joyfully loved by God, so we will be able to offer something of that same love to our children, and point them ultimately to the one who loves them more than we will ever be able to.

**Prayer**

*Dear Father, thank you that by your Spirit, you have adopted us into your family. Thank you that you love us, and accept us as we are, and think the best of us. Please help us to offer that same kind of steadfast love to our children, and heal us of everything that would stop us doing so. In Jesus' name we pray. Amen*

# Deep-rooted strength

**Ephesians 3:14–21 (NRSV)**

For this reason I bow my knees before the Father, from whom every family in heaven and on earth takes its name. I pray that, according to the riches of his glory, he may grant that you may be strengthened in your inner being with power through his Spirit, and that Christ may dwell in your hearts through faith, as you are being rooted and grounded in love. I pray that you may have the power to comprehend, with all the saints, what is the breadth and length and height and depth, and to know the love of Christ that surpasses knowledge, so that you may be filled with all the fullness of God.

Now to him who by the power at work within us is able to accomplish abundantly far more than all we can ask or imagine, to him be glory in the church and in Christ Jesus to all generations, forever and ever. Amen.

Paul's prayer here for the Ephesians is one which should encourage us at any time. It is possibly a passage that you have referred to several times before, and the kind of passage that you may want to read twice, as it makes you feel 'yes please, Lord'! It is particularly pertinent at times in our lives when we are aware of our need for God and his presence. During the time after the birth of a child, we may feel like that. We feel drained and empty, both physically and emotionally, and in need of something extra.

The challenges that we face as new parents, and the adjustments that we have to make, can bring us greater awareness of our need for God's help than ever before. As we recognize that we cannot do this alone, so we are driven back to God.

When you were preparing for the birth of your child, you probably had to do breathing exercises, so that in labour, when the pressure was on, you could use what you had learnt to aid the delivery. Usually the father and mother are encouraged to do this together. The man does not have to take deep breaths himself to ease the birth, but in doing so, or in reminding his partner to do so, his contribution is important.

In the same way, when we face added pressure on our lives, we may sometimes have to prompt our partners to take time out with God. When there is so much to do, a few minutes spent quietly with God can be the first thing to go out of the window. We may even feel that it is self-indulgent to try to maintain this habit. To give each other permission to take this time out can be a valuable way of supporting and standing alongside each other.

It isn't easy to be concerned with other people's needs when we feel ourselves to be under pressure. We are tempted to dwell on our own needs and struggles to the exclusion of all else. In a family, one partner who stays at home may feel that (s)he bears all the stress of the demanding new child, while the partner who goes to work feels that (s)he is the one on whom the pressure really falls. When we feel like this, we end up protecting ourselves instead of supporting each other. In his letter to the Ephesians, Paul demonstrates that he knew how to stand alongside people, even when he faced great pressure himself. At the time of writing, he was in prison, but his concern was for the people he wrote to. We need to imitate him in our relationships with one another. That may mean encouraging your partner to take some time out each day, not when they are nursing a sleeping or suckling baby, but to have some space alone with God. You may also have to ask them for that same support, for example by asking them to take the child so that you can have some undisturbed time. This may not be long—even five minutes a day can help.

As a new mother or father, we face new challenges and demands on us. Paul directs us back to God the Father, our father who provides for our needs. Paul prays that the Ephesians 'may be strengthened in your inner being with power through his Spirit' (v. 16). From deep within, there can be a knowledge and peace which come only from God. As parents of a young child, we may feel as if there is never any space or peace for ourselves. This may be literally true at times because of constant crying or other 'baby noises'. We can feel trapped by noise and demands which over a prolonged period may leave us feeling desperate. I have lost count of the number of nights that I have gone to bed in urgent need of a good night's sleep only to be woken at 1 a.m.,

3 a.m. and 4.30 a.m., and finally having to get up at 6 a.m. because I could not stand it any more. Feeling like this, it is even more difficult to ask God for anything, let alone to strengthen your inner self. However, when we look at verses 16 and 17 from this passage in Ephesians, we are reminded that at these times God is keen and eager to meet with us and work in us. God's hand on our life and the resources that he gives us to deal with our daily routine are the ways in which he ministers to us.

Paul's second prayer is that 'Christ may dwell in your hearts through faith, as you are being rooted and grounded in love' (v. 17). As we begin to rely on God's Spirit to empower us, we will become more rooted and grounded in Christ's love. God pours his love into us, assuring us of his love for us, and enabling us to give love to others.

When we become parents, a new dimension opens up in our ability to love. We don't love those around us any less, but a deep reservoir of love is generated which seems able to incorporate love for the new child without detracting from our previous loves. This is true however many children we have. When we love someone, our motivation is more likely to be right in the things that we do for them. This doesn't mean that we become a doormat. It is a tough love, which enables us to encourage others to develop to the best of their ability, even to challenge them when necessary. This may be true in our relationship with our husband or wife when we have to 'lovingly encourage' them to share in changing nappies or getting up in the night. It will also be true in our relationship with our new child, if not now, then in the future.

The knowledge of the love of Christ that Paul goes on to speak about is beyond our normal experience. It was because of his love and compassion for us that Christ died. His love is sacrificial love, which pinned him to the cross more effectively than nails ever could. As we begin to have an idea of the love that Christ has for us, then the awesomeness of God becomes more apparent. We will be able to receive from and be empowered by what God has to give us as we understand this love.

As a parent, our love for our child is never going to be greater than the love of God for him or her. We are still frail and human, and as much as we love, God's love is greater. When we pray for our children, we may feel that because of our love we are pleading with God to do what is best for our loved ones. In reality, it is God who loves the best, and who wants the best for our children.

The summer when Jacqui took her A' Levels she did some work on a Christian holiday camp with several of her schoolfriends, and she was there when the exam results came out. Although her friends had all done extremely well, and had easily gained admission to their chosen universities, Jacqui had not. There was no way that she could go to the university she wanted to, and she was devastated. A few days later, Jacqui's dad was driving up to see her. As he drove, he was praying about what to say to his tearful daughter, who at that stage was feeling as if her whole future had collapsed in front of her. Dad, not normally one for direct revelation from God, felt the Lord saying to him that although he was Jacqui's earthly father and wanted what was best for her, God as her heavenly Father knew what really was best. If we had a penny for every time that Dad has subsequently told this story, we would be rich! But it was true. If Jacqui had not gone to Portsmouth Polytechnic, she would never have met Stephen! God's hand was on her life for the best, even when she felt that it was not.

Today, may the prayer of Paul for the Ephesians be the basis for your prayers for yourself and for your family. Reread the passage as a personal prayer for you and your family, that he may strengthen you, and reveal to you more of the riches of his love.

# Be gentle with yourself

**Matthew 11:28–30 (NRSV)**

'Come to me, all you that are weary and are carrying heavy burdens, and I will give you rest. Take my yoke upon you, and learn from me; for I am gentle and humble in heart, and you will find rest for your souls. For my yoke is easy, and my burden is light.'

The new pressures that we face as we become parents can be incredibly daunting. We have to learn new skills and develop others that do not necessarily come naturally to us in order to deal with our new child. It may also be a time when our natural resources are at a very low ebb, due to lack of sleep and the physical demands of childbirth, from which it can take some time to recover. Some people seem to thrive in these conditions, but most of us do not.

When we are feeling physically tired, the tasks that we previously considered everyday and routine may become marginalized or even be skipped altogether. This can lead us to feel a sense of failure as we are unable to meet our own expectations of ourselves. We may also feel that we are letting our partner down, as we are unable to maintain the areas of our joint life which have previously been our responsibility. For example, giving up work or taking unpaid paternity leave may have led to a drastic cut in our income, so creating new pressures. Alternatively we may feel guilty about the reduced amount of housework that we are now able to do. Whatever the issue is for us, it can make us feel down on ourselves.

In the past few readings, we have looked at ways in which God provides us with the resources that we need to cope with these new challenges. His Holy Spirit within us can bring us peace and help us to know his grace. But God knows that it is hard. God understands the struggles that we face each day when we feel run down and exhausted, and he has no desire to send us on a guilt trip on top of all that. In today's reading from Matthew, Jesus draws those who are tired and weary to himself. He offers support and comfort. He does not challenge us about why we are unable to cope, he does not quiz us on our routine, or what we should or should not be doing. He wants to meet us at our point of need: that is, he offers us rest.

Jesus is there for us if we are worn down with the pressures of being a parent. He is not there to condemn us, but rather to stand alongside us. I doubt whether Jesus is too concerned if we bottle- or breast-feed. He probably does not have strong opinions either on feeding on demand or making the child wait three hours, or on where our baby sleeps, be it in her own room, in a cot, or in bed with us. Everyone else you meet may seem to have views or opinions on these issues, particularly if they are parents themselves, but Jesus' primary concern is for us and our child as individuals. In this passage in Matthew, he is offering unconditional rest for those who are weary and heavy-laden, and this applies to us as new parents as least as much as anyone else.

So do not be too hard on yourself. As Jesus offers rest to the weary, then maybe we should take up his offer. It is vital for your health and well-being that you take time out for yourself. Just as, in order to maintain our relationship with God, we need to take time out to be with him, it is also necessary and important to allow time for yourself. Initially this may be just to catch up on some sleep, but it is a valuable habit to sit down with a cup of tea and draw breath for half an hour when the baby sleeps. There will always be jobs that need doing, but even if you get them all done there will always be more. At home, Jacqui jokes about the fact that whenever she manages to empty the laundry basket (not something that happens very often), someone spills something, or worse, within the hour. It is a never-ending battle and it will not go away, whether it is the laundry, the ironing, the hoovering, dusting, sweeping, or whatever. (In our house, all of the above apply!) So sometimes, we all have to stop. This may be a hard discipline to learn, but at the end of the day it is worth it. Even God, when he had finished his work of creation, stopped to rest (Genesis 2:2). We need to do the same.

To be effective in this, we also need to be gentle on our partners, to support them and encourage them to take time for themselves, and to experience the rest that Jesus offers. This may mean not always dumping the baby on your partner as soon as he or she gets in from a day's work and saying, 'I've had him all day, now it's your turn', but allowing them space too. Or it may mean getting in from work, picking up the baby and sending your partner for a rest! For each of us it will be different, and it will inevitably mean changes from how things were before. But if you can get used to supporting each other through this stage, then you are providing one of the most valuable resources of all, that comfort and recuperating rest that Jesus offers to those who need it.

Because it requires us to learn how to balance and prioritize what is important in our everyday lives, adapting to parenting is best worked at together as a couple. We need to watch out for the needs and pressure points in our own and our partner's life and change together to accommodate life with a new baby. We may need to encourage each other to participate in the new chores that it entails, like nappy changing and bath-time, but we also have a responsibility to protect personal time for both of us. Jesus recognized that we need rest when we are weary. We can recognize that same need in each other, and make sure it is met.

**Prayer**

*Dear Lord Jesus, thank you that you offer rest to the weary. Thank you that you care much more about who we are than about what we can do. Please help us as we juggle with the different areas of our lives, to remember to take time for ourselves, so that we may feel rested and refreshed each day. Amen*

# Trust for the future

**Luke 1:28–38 (NRSV)**

The angel came to Mary and said, 'Greetings, favoured one! The Lord is with you.' But she was much perplexed by his words and pondered what sort of greeting this might be. The angel said to her, 'Do not be afraid, Mary, for you have found favour with God. And now, you will conceive in your womb and bear a son, and you will name him Jesus. He will be great, and will be called the Son of the Most High, and the Lord God will give to him the throne of his ancestor David. He will reign over the house of Jacob forever, and of his kingdom there will be no end.'

Mary said to the angel, 'How can this be, since I am a virgin?' The angel said to her, 'The Holy Spirit will come upon you, and the power of the Most High will overshadow you; therefore the child to be born will be holy; he will be called Son of God. And now, your relative Elizabeth in her old age has also conceived a son; and this is the sixth month for her who was said to be barren. For nothing will be impossible with God.' Then Mary said, 'Here am I, the servant of the Lord; let it be with me according to your word.' Then the angel departed from her.

The angel Gabriel visited Mary and informed her that she was the one. She was going to be the mother of the Messiah for whom the Jews had been waiting. It was every young girl's dream to be chosen by God to be the mother of the Saviour of the Jews and it was happening to her. Wow! As with so many dreams, they sound a great idea on paper, but the reality can be somewhat more daunting. Mary, engaged to be married to a respectable carpenter, risked losing everything. In those days, a single mother had no chance of surviving on her own, and there was no guarantee that Joseph, her husband-to-be, would stick by her. Gabriel did not add, '...and I am just off to clear this with Joseph'. From the moment that the angel told Mary that she was the one, she had to trust in God completely in the midst of her uncertainty about the future.

Mary seemed to take it completely in her stride. Her first thoughts were not about how awkward a social situation she was being put into, nor how difficult it would be to explain this pregnancy to Joseph. She was not upset because the timing was not what she would have chosen herself. She accepted the situation. Although the means of conception had to be explained to her, Mary was willing to take on that responsibility for a new life which God had given to her, whatever the personal cost. Her response was to worship and praise God for the privilege he had given to her, and to trust him for the future.

In our case, the challenge of parenting a new child is not quite so directly God-given as it was with Mary and Joseph. We are more likely to be told that a child is on the way by a blue line in a pregnancy test than by an angelic visitation. However, all life is ordained by God, and that is true whether or not we consciously planned to bring this child into the world. He still entrusts us with that responsibility for a new life which he has given. It is something which should not be taken lightly, as it will affect us and our children for the rest of our lives. How we handle that responsibility will dictate how we cope with parenting as the months and years go by.

If you have become a parent recently, particularly if this is for the first time, you are probably all too well aware of the challenges that lie ahead. In the past few readings, we have been looking at some of the resources that God willingly gives us to help us cope with the pressures and changes that a new child brings. We hope that as you have considered these resources, you have been reassured that you are not alone in this.

We may face a difficult time. Our minds may be filled with worries about how we are going to cope physically or emotionally or how we will manage financially. These are real, genuine concerns that can affect the quality of our life. In the hours and days following the angel's visit, Mary must have wondered about some of these things too. But we can learn from Mary's example to trust in God both with the little things and with the big things in our lives.

The points at which we need to seek God's help consciously for ourselves will differ for each of us. For example, Jacqui often battles with sleeplessness. She has lost count of the nights spent lying awake, worrying about the fact that she cannot sleep. But when she calms down enough to ask God for his peace and rest, then peace comes. For you the problem may be different. Whatever it may be, God's resources are available to help.

It may be that sometimes God has to strip away everything else, so that we can rely on him and trust in his provision for us and our family. When the angel left Mary, he left her with the possibility that in human terms she had no future. There was no guarantee that Joseph would stand by her, and no social services to cling on to (and I would not have fancied her chances with the Child Support Agency!) However, left with the angel's words that 'nothing will be impossible with God' (v. 37), Mary was prepared to trust in God completely for her future and that of her child.

When Natalie was six weeks old, we had to move house, from Nottingham, where we had friends and relatives close by, to Portsmouth, where we hardly knew anyone. Although Stephen had moved around the country a lot as a child, Jacqui had lived in the same village from the time she was born until she left home to go to college, so she was convinced that this was a particularly big deal! Also, Jacqui was the one who had to comfort the unsettled baby as, over four nights, we slept in four different beds! Although she was excited at the prospect of a new home as we started life as a family, she was also apprehensive about what the future would hold. One evening during our first week in our new home, we headed down to the sea front. It was dark and the lights were on along the promenade and the pier. In front of us lay the expanse of the sea (well, ten miles of it before the Isle of Wight). We could hear the waves breaking on the pebbles on the beach, and smell the salt water in the air. Somehow, we knew that everything would be all right. We knew God's presence with us then, and his hand upon our lives. When everything else was taken away from us, we had to rely on God and his provision for our life. That was enough to see us through.

**Prayer**

*Dear Lord, however I feel today, help me to trust in you. May I know your strength and resources as I go about my day, and may I now and in the future trust in you, even when everything else may seem hard. I ask this in Jesus' name. Amen*

# A heritage of faith

**2 Timothy 1:3–5 (NRSV)**

I am grateful to God—whom I worship with a clear conscience, as my ancestors did—when I remember you constantly in my prayers night and day. Recalling your tears, I long to see you so that I may be filled with joy. I am reminded of your sincere faith, a faith that lived first in your grandmother Lois and your mother Eunice and now, I am sure, lives in you.

In the next set of readings, we are going to be thinking about some of the changes that have to take place in our lifestyle when a child is born. By now you are probably painfully aware of the ways in which your life has had to change. You have had to slow down and alter your expectations of what you can achieve in a day. Your priorities may be different than previously. Things that seemed straightforward in the past have suddenly become stressful jobs. At the time of writing, I have just spent my first night alone with three children. In order to arrive at school by 9.00 a.m. I had to organize clothes the night before and run our morning routine more like a military campaign. The birth of a child makes the simplest task a daunting challenge.

As we begin this section, we look at a reading which emphasizes the influence and potential importance of a Christian family. In verse 3, Paul speaks about the God whom he worships 'as (his) ancestors did'. The best start in life that any of us can give our children is bringing them up in a Christian home, with Christian principles and morals. This background of faith and love established early in a life will influence the child's future and the way in which they think and react to things as they grow.

When Paul writes to Timothy, he stresses the importance of Timothy's heritage of faith. It is a background that he should be proud of, as both his mother and grandmother were women of deep spirituality. Often, you can see faith being passed down the generations of a family, and the support of a Christian family has often been a vital ingredient in the lives of influential Christian leaders and thinkers.

The foundations of a Christian faith can be established before a child is born, as we begin to pray for our unborn child. This can then develop into prayer for our baby, toddler, schoolchild, teenager, right through to adulthood, but the sooner it begins the better. It is never too early (or too late) to begin to pray for your children.

As the mother of a young baby, I spend a reasonably large amount of time sitting, either feeding or nursing a sleeping or sleepy baby. (I have yet to find a foolproof method of putting a sleeping baby to bed during the day without waking them up in the process. Suggestions on a postcard please!) Although by temperament I like to be constantly on the go, usually with a long list of urgent jobs in my mind or written down somewhere, having a young baby insists that I put a stop to that. Some things just cannot get done. Although this can be frustrating, it is possible to make a virtue of necessity, because this time during which I am otherwise incapacitated does give me a unique opportunity to pray or to read, and if I use the time wisely I can establish good foundations in prayer for my child's future.

Holding a sleeping or feeding baby can add inspiration to our prayer life. This can be particularly helpful when we are so tired that we find it difficult to string words into coherent sentences. It gives us a visual illustration of how God protects and cares for us and our child. The sound of the baby breathing can inspire prayers about their health and future growth. The sight of the baby curled up asleep on a parent may focus prayers for future security and contentment. You can develop your own prayers based on the needs and character of your baby and your situation. Your time spent nursing your child does not have to be a time when you are feeling guilty about all the other things that need to be done. Instead it can be a time when you are laying the foundations of their Christian heritage as you pray for them, your family and the future. At times it can also be an opportunity for you to sleep or watch television.

I find that when I am awake feeding during the night, it is a good time to pray for my family and friends and about things that are troubling me. These prayers are not wordy or articulate, but I use the time to commit to God situations that I know about. You will need to find your own prayer times that fit in with your lifestyle. As a new parent, this will quite possibly be different from the time before you had children. Over the weeks, you will be able to develop your own pattern for prayer, but at the beginning of any child's life, whether it is your first, second, third or fourth baby, any type of routine is hard to maintain. It is always difficult to change from a prayer routine which may have been established for a long time. But it may encourage us to make the effort when we remember how important our prayers for our child can be.

If you are the only parent committed to bringing your child up as a Christian, either because your partner is not a Christian or because you are a single parent, then this passage from Timothy can be a particular encouragement to you. Paul only mentions Timothy's mother and grandmother. He makes no reference at all to his father or grandfather. It was the faith and example of his mother and grandmother that had established the depth of commitment in Timothy. So if you are the only Christian parent, the best grounding that you can give your son or daughter is by demonstrating Christian principles and practice yourself. However, as Timothy's mother had the support of his grandmother, both you and your child will be aided in this if you have other mature Christians to stand with you as foundation-builders for your child. If you belong to a Christian tradition which makes use of godparents, these people, if carefully chosen, may give you the support you need. If your child does not have godparents, it may be helpful to find other Christians who will commit themselves to support and pray for your child.

**Prayer**

*Dear Lord, as I adjust to the changes in my life demanded by the birth of my child, teach me how to pray for him/her. Teach me how to show my children the joy of faith which is their heritage. I ask that you would teach me how to pray in new ways. Amen*

# Getting the foundations right

**1 Chronicles 29:10–19 (NRSV)**

Then David blessed the Lord in the presence of all the assembly; David said: 'Blessed are you, O Lord, the God of our ancestor Israel, forever and ever. Yours, O Lord, are the greatness, the power, the glory, the victory, and the majesty; for all that is in the heavens and on the earth is yours; yours is the kingdom, O Lord, and you are exalted as head above all. Riches and honour come from you, and you rule over all. In your hand are power and might; and it is in your hand to make great and to give strength to all. And now, our God, we give thanks to you and praise your glorious name.

'But who am I, and what is my people, that we should be able to make this freewill offering? For all things come from you, and of your own have we given you. For we are aliens and transients before you, as were all our ancestors; our days on the earth are like a shadow, and there is no hope. O Lord our God, all this abundance that we have provided for building you a house for your holy name comes from your hand and is all your own. I know, my God, that you search the heart, and take pleasure in uprightness; in the uprightness of my heart I have freely offered all these things, and now I have seen your people, who are present here, offering freely and joyously to you. O Lord, the God of Abraham, Isaac, and Israel, our ancestors, keep forever such purposes and thoughts in the hearts of your people, and direct their hearts toward you. Grant to my son Solomon that with single mind he may keep your commandments, your decrees, and your statutes, performing all of them, and that he may build the temple for which I have made provision.'

King David was coming to the end of his life. He knew that his time was almost over, that soon the throne of Israel would pass to his son

Solomon. It was no secret that his life had been a chequered affair, with moments of triumph and success, and times of failure and despair. But as he looked back over the years that he had led Israel, he saw the faithfulness of God at work in the good times and the bad times alike.

Our own experience is often similar. Sometimes we feel full of energy, masters of our own lives, successful in all we do. Other times we feel depleted and worn out, weak and sinful, and we wonder how we're ever going to get back on top of life again. Neither feelings of euphoria nor feelings of failure are necessarily accurate assessments of our lives. It's only as we look back over a longer period of time that we see where the successes and the failures have truly been. It's in looking back, too, that we become aware of God's faithful provision for us, year in, year out.

At the time of writing, we are preparing to move to another church in a new area. Time is running out in our present place of ministry. Yet there are still things we would like to achieve and make secure in the weeks that are left to us. David felt like that too. He was concerned about two things in particular.

First of all, he was passionate about the temple. David had long wanted to build a temple for the worship of the Lord, but God had spoken to him through a prophet and forbidden it. David had no doubt experienced that disappointment that all of us face when we realize that some long-cherished goal is never going to be achieved, at least not by us. But he had come to terms with that, and instead he had done as much as he could to make the task straightforward for the next king, his son Solomon. He had collected the gold and the jewels together, purchased the wood and the iron, and called on the people to commit themselves to the task. All that David could do without actually building, he had done. He had laid the foundations for Solomon to build upon, metaphorically speaking.

All of us who are parents need to lay foundations for our children to build upon. Presumably few of us contemplate leaving building projects for our children to complete. But in all sorts of other ways we are giving our children foundations on which to build. They may be foundations of security and self-confidence, or of fear of failure and low self-esteem. They may be foundations of trust in God, or of reliance on human wisdom. We need to continually ask ourselves, 'What sort of foundations am I laying for my child's future life?'

Secondly, David was passionate about Solomon himself. He had experienced the heartache of seeing some of his children go off the rails. His family life had generally been something of a mess. All his hopes were now founded upon this young man who was to succeed him. The future of his family and his kingdom rested on Solomon. So in this act of public worship that our reading describes, he prayed for Solomon, that God would give to him the resources and character qualities that he needed to serve God and his people wholeheartedly.

Why did David pray for Solomon? Why is it important for us to cultivate the habit of prayer for our children? There are at least three reasons we might think of.

First of all, *prayer changes things*. As we pray for someone or something, we begin to see answers to our prayers. The story is often told of the mother of Augustine, who prayed year after year that her son would abandon his immoral lifestyle and turn to God. Long after most of us would have given up, she kept on praying, until Augustine was powerfully converted. He became one of the strongest influences in the developing church.

Secondly, *prayer changes us*. As we pray for someone, we begin to see that person from God's point of view. We also begin to see the world from their point of view. If we want to understand what is really happening in our child's life, prayer is the best place to start.

Thirdly, *prayer changes God*, or at least it may change his actions. Genesis 18 tells the story of Abraham bargaining with God for the city of Sodom. God is portrayed as rethinking his plan in the light of Abraham's petitions. Whilst God's character and overall purpose for the world are unchanging, he may change what he does in a particular situation in response to prayer. Or, to look at it from another angle, God's best plan may be implemented only in response to prayer.

Many of the adjustments we make as parents are difficult, but the small changes can be the most important. Whatever else we may struggle with, we can decide to lay firm foundations for our children, by the example we set, and by daily prayer for them.

**Prayer**

*Lord God, thank you that as we look back over the years we can see your faithful provision for us. Please help us to be faithful parents, in the example we set, and in daily prayer for our children. Amen*

# Great expectations

**1 Samuel 16:13–22 (NRSV)**

Then Samuel took the horn of oil, and anointed him in the presence of his brothers; and the spirit of the Lord came mightily upon David from that day forward. Samuel then set out and went to Ramah.

Now the spirit of the Lord departed from Saul, and an evil spirit from the Lord tormented him. And Saul's servants said to him, 'See now, an evil spirit from God is tormenting you. Let our lord now command the servants who attend you to look for someone who is skilful in playing the lyre; and when the evil spirit from God is upon you, he will play it, and you will feel better.' So Saul said to his servants, 'Provide for me someone who can play well, and bring him to me.' One of the young men answered, 'I have seen a son of Jesse the Bethlehemite who is skilful in playing, a man of valour, a warrior, prudent in speech, and a man of good presence; and the Lord is with him.' So Saul sent messengers to Jesse, and said, 'Send me your son David who is with the sheep.' Jesse took a donkey loaded with bread, a skin of wine, and a kid, and sent them by his son David to Saul. And David came to Saul, and entered his service. Saul loved him greatly, and he became his armour-bearer. Saul sent to Jesse, saying, 'Let David remain in my service, for he has found favour in my sight.'

What are your hopes for your children? What ambitions or expectations do you have for them as they grow up? Academic brilliance, a warm family life, a successful career, are just a few of the things that parents dream of when they envisage their child's adult life.

Sometimes our hopes for our children may be unrealistically ambitious. If every desire we have had for ours is fulfilled, expect to see both the country and the church led by the Hance dynasty some time in the new century! High hopes on the part of the parents can be crippling for the child as she grows up. Some parents dream that their child will be the first in the family to go to university, or will continue the family tradition of an army officer in every generation. These ambitions may make a child feel constrained or trapped, unable to please Mum and Dad without sacrificing his own desires.

Other parents positively resist any attempt by their children to be outstanding in any field. We recently overheard a conversation outside the school gates in which one mother was explaining to another her hopes for her daughter. 'I just want her to be average,' she said, 'not the best in the class, not the worst in the class, just average.' We were shocked by such a lack of hope for this little girl to fulfil her potential.

It can be hard for parents to cope when it appears that their hopes for their children are not going to be fulfilled. Signs of early promise that never seem to come to anything, or real potential which goes undeveloped in an adolescent rebellious phase, can cause real heartache which any of us may have to face. Although most typically we may expect to have to deal with this issue when our child is a teenager or older, even in the early years we may experience disappointment with our child's development in some areas. But today's Bible reading offers us hope on three counts.

First of all, we see from the example of David that children are often multi-gifted. That is, there may be more than one area in which they have talents and abilities, and the area that their parents focus on and seek to develop may not be the one which ultimately will be most significant.

David was firstly a shepherd. He was probably a very good shepherd. We know that he was courageous in defending his flock against predators (1 Samuel 17:34–37), so his father Jesse presumably thought he did a fine job. Perhaps Jesse dreamt of David becoming a great shepherd, the best his family had yet produced. Yet that dream was to go unfulfilled.

David had another outstanding ability. He was a gifted musician. Not only could he play, but he had a depth to his playing which enabled him to soothe the most anguished of listeners. So skilled was he that his talent brought him to the notice of King Saul. If Jesse was a typical father he could have died happy at that point. Here was his son, a shepherd from the middle of nowhere, playing music for the king. What higher aspiration could a musician possibly have?

But of course, David had another set of attributes—courage,

wisdom, humility before God—which would take him out of the shepherding business and even out of the music business for good, and make him king. The gifts that Jesse saw in him were not the gifts he used for his life's work.

Secondly, this passage reminds us that the path to the fulfilment of a person's potential does not always run straight. In 1 Samuel 16, David is anointed king. What happens after that? Does he travel, amidst public acclamation, to his royal palace and begin to reign? No, he goes back to the sheep. God's calling upon his life was not fulfilled for some time.

When Stephen was seventeen years old, he felt that God was calling him to ordained ministry in the Church of England. Immediately, he began to act upon this call, contacting the relevant people, having meetings with bishops and others. Yet ten years passed before his ordination, of which he was in training for only three.

Your child, or my child, may have some particular vocation, some work or service to which they are called and suited. At some point it may become clear what that calling is. Yet many years may pass before they are working in that field. The path to the fulfilment of a person's potential does not always run straight.

Finally, the passage reminds us that God is involved in all of this. True, we are never specifically told that God is working out his purpose behind the scenes, and yet that is the unspoken assumption of the whole narrative. It is God who anoints David for kingship to come, God who allows Saul's torment and God who relieves that torment when David plays. It is God who will ultimately remove Saul as king and place the kingdom in David's hands. Throughout the story God is at work, fulfilling his purposes for David and Israel.

As we look at our lives, the path seldom seems to run straight, and as we watch our children grow up and take their own paths the same will be true. Yet as we seek God's will, for ourselves and them, we begin to see how he is working his purposes out. His dreams for our children may differ from ours, but whilst our ambitions for them may constrict them, his never will, because he knows them and loves them better than we ever could.

**Prayer**

*Almighty God, as we look to our children's future, may our dreams for them be in line with your will. Please help them to fulfil their potential and to develop into the people you want them to be, knowing and loving you as their Lord and Saviour. Amen*

# The principle of partnership

**Genesis 2:18–24 (NRSV)**

Then the Lord God said, 'It is not good that the man should be alone; I will make him a helper as his partner.' So out of the ground the Lord God formed every animal of the field and every bird of the air, and brought them to the man to see what he would call them; and whatever the man called every living creature, that was its name. The man gave names to all cattle, and to the birds of the air, and to every animal of the field; but for the man there was not found a helper as his partner. So the Lord God caused a deep sleep to fall upon the man, and he slept; then he took one of his ribs and closed up its place with flesh. And the rib that the Lord God had taken from the man he made into a woman and brought her to the man. Then the man said, 'This at last is bone of my bones and flesh of my flesh; this one shall be called Woman, for out of Man this one was taken.'

Therefore a man leaves his father and his mother and clings to his wife, and they become one flesh.

As his creator, God gave the man the job of naming the animals. This policy has not been one that we have followed. Jacqui has chosen the first names of all our children, with Stephen being allowed his say for their middle names only! We have always eventually reached a common viewpoint about names and then tried to live with our decision for a few weeks before the baby was due, just to make sure that we could get used to it. Although we have always chosen names because we liked them, we have also always investigated their meaning before we have made our final decision. The choosing of a name is very important, and it is a big responsibility to name someone else who will have to put up with that choice for life.

When God told Adam to name the animals, he had an ulterior motive. God knew that on his own Adam would be lonely. Adam needed a friend, a companion, and this gave him the opportunity to find one.

However, in the animal kingdom no suitable partner could be found. In some cases it may be true that 'a man's best friend is his dog' but this relationship can never be one of equals. God needed to find for Adam an equal partner to share in his responsibilities and lifestyle. So God created woman.

This passage from Genesis emphasizes the importance of the partnership of the man and the woman. It is about a relationship of equals, and if anyone is in any doubt about that, the author of Genesis describes how 'a man leaves his father and his mother and clings to his wife' (v. 24). He is neither superior nor inferior to her, but he needs her, he 'clings' to her. The man and the woman are dependent on each other to function at their best. This passage tells us about the principle of partnership. It tells not only of God's plan to make a suitable helper for the man but also of the man's dependence on the woman. The woman was created to be the man's helper and companion as his equal to share in the work that God had given him.

As partners and parents, it is vital for us to take on a variety of roles at different times. When we have a new baby, the different jobs that we are required to carry out within our partnership may change rapidly. If one partner has given up work to care for the child (either permanently or for the short-term) then there is an obvious shift in responsibility, and one which both parents may find very difficult to adjust to.

Anyone who stops doing paid work and stays at home to care for a child has to struggle with the implications of no longer bringing in a wage. However understanding and supportive your partner is, there is an adjustment to make. For many families, living on one income leaves the financial situation tight, and if you no longer bring any money into the house it is hard not to feel guilty about it. At the same time we live in a society where the person that we are is defined by the job that we do. Therefore it can be difficult to admit that your job is that of 'homemaker' or whatever you choose to call yourself. (I have one friend who describes herself as a 'domestic slave'.) But there can be no more valuable contribution to family life and society than to provide a safe and secure environment in which children can grow up, develop, and explore. After all, you are shaping the next generation.

For a parent who has to return to work after maternity or paternity leave, there are other difficulties to come to terms with. It is easy to feel that you are missing out on your son or daughter's development when you are at work all day, or to feel a little jealous of the primary carer's relationship with him or her. It is vital to realize that your contribution to family life is just as important as that of the person who cares for the child. A family needs resources to live on, and if you are bringing money into the home then you are freeing up someone else to concentrate on the needs and development of your baby (whether that is your husband or wife or a paid carer.)

Throughout the adjustments and changes in lifestyle that are demanded of us when we have a new baby, it is most important that we continue to function as an equal partnership. Adapting to leaving work, or returning to work when we are struggling because of a shortage of sleep, is incredibly difficult. At this time of changing roles we often feel insecure in ourselves and need to look to our partners for reassurance and support. It is therefore imperative that we look at our husband or wife not as superior or inferior to ourselves, but as an equal partner as we both fulfil the jobs that we have undertaken at this stage in our lives.

**Prayer**

*Heavenly Father, thank you that you did not design us to live or function in isolation. Thank you for the support that we have through partnership and friendship. Please help us to develop and encourage each other in our changing roles. Amen*

# Different gifts, one family

**1 Corinthians 12:4–7, 14–20 (NRSV)**

Now there are varieties of gifts, but the same Spirit; and there are varieties of services, but the same Lord; and there are varieties of activities, but it is the same God who activates all of them in everyone. To each is given the manifestation of the Spirit for the common good...

Indeed, the body does not consist of one member but of many. If the foot would say, 'Because I am not a hand, I do not belong to the body,' that would not make it any less a part of the body. And if the ear would say, 'Because I am not an eye, I do not belong to the body,' that would not make it any less a part of the body. If the whole body were an eye, where would the hearing be? If the whole body were hearing, where would the sense of smell be? But as it is, God arranged the members in the body, each one of them, as he chose. If all were a single member, where would the body be? As it is, there are many members, yet one body.

In the church of today, we are used to hearing people talk about 'every-member ministry'. Many churches have been liberated by the realization that ministry is not the prerogative of the pastor or vicar, or even a select group of leaders, but is the work of the entire church. Passages such as the one we have just read remind us that God has given gifts and abilities to every Christian, not just a favoured few.

One church to which we belonged summed this up in the slogan 'Everybody doing one thing well'. The idea was that each church member would find his or her niche in church life, and then get on with serving in that area. That way we would avoid having a handful of overworked, burned-out people doing all the work, while a larger number of pew-fillers attended on Sunday but did nothing else.

The key to making every-member ministry work is in helping each person to work out what his or her gifts are. Only when we are clear about what talents and abilities God has given us, or is giving us, to be used for the good of the whole, can we begin to sharpen up and use those gifts effectively.

The local church is often likened to a family, with lessons learned in the home applied to the congregation. But that process can work in reverse, too. The Bible's teaching about the gifts that God gives to the church can also be applied, to some extent, to our lives as families. So, in the same way that effective and happy service in the church begins with discerning the gifts of each individual, it can also be helpful to establish what gifts each person in our family or household is able to offer.

Some of these gifts may be personality traits. One child has the ability to make us laugh at exactly the moment when tension needs to be alleviated. One parent has the patience to keep his or her temper when other people might lose it. A family unit works well when the combinations of gifts and characteristics complement each other. Sometimes we may need to ask God to give us these gifts when we know our family life requires them.

But in the widest sense, our gifts are also to do with what we do in the family, with the contribution we make to our life together. For a parent who has given up work to stay at home, this may be a gift of time which is made available to the whole family—time to listen, to care, to read stories, to talk. For another parent who is working, this may be a gift of providing for the family's material needs. To provide a warm home, food on the table and clothes to wear is a wonderful and vital gift. For another parent who has returned to work and pays for child-care, this in itself may be their gift. Some women, particularly, may go through life feeling guilty that they have chosen this course, even though the children are growing up secure and cared-for and happy. This of course doesn't free us from the responsibility parents have to love and care for their children. There are some things that we cannot employ other people to do.

Paul, in the passage we read today, was insistent that each person's gift was valuable, and that there was no guilt to be attached to having one gift rather than another. Some parents need to hear this. Some parents feel guilty that they go to work and aren't at home all day, without realizing what a huge contribution they are making. Others feel guilty that they are at home all day, and no longer contribute to the family income. Some parents experience guilt because they don't feel that parenting comes naturally to them at all, but rather they have to work at it, and may feel drained by it. They imagine that other parents are gifted in a way that they are not.

The important thing is to recognize what our gift is, and to value it. Just as important is to recognize what our spouse contributes, and value that too.

A word of warning, though. This analogy is not perfect. In even a small church, there are many more people than in the largest family. There is scope for specialisation that no family has. Parenting makes generalists of us all. It isn't a good enough excuse to say, 'I can't change a nappy, darling, it's not my gift.' There are some skills that we simply have to learn, whether they come naturally to us or not. But once we have recognized the gifts that we do have, and learned to value them, we are in a better position to learn to do some of the things we find difficult, knowing that whilst we may be weak in some areas, we are strong in others, and our family functions better as a result.

**Prayer**

*Dear God, thank you that by your Holy Spirit you have given each of us gifts for the good of others. Please help us in our family to recognize our own gifts, and the gifts of each other, and to value them. Amen*

# Precious memories

**Luke 2:41–52 (NRSV)**

Now every year his parents went to Jerusalem for the festival of the Passover. And when he was twelve years old, they went up as usual for the festival. When the festival was ended and they started to return, the boy Jesus stayed behind in Jerusalem, but his parents did not know it. Assuming that he was in the group of travellers, they went a day's journey. Then they started to look for him among their relatives and friends. When they did not find him, they returned to Jerusalem to search for him. After three days they found him in the temple, sitting among the teachers, listening to them and asking them questions. And all who heard him were amazed at his understanding and his answers. When his parents saw him they were astonished; and his mother said to him, 'Child, why have you treated us like this? Look, your father and I have been searching for you in great anxiety.' He said to them, 'Why were you searching for me? Did you not know that I must be in my Father's house?' But they did not understand what he said to them.Then he went down with them and came to Nazareth, and was obedient to them. His mother treasured all these things in her heart.

And Jesus increased in wisdom and in years, and in divine and human favour.

In the current climate, when we do not like to leave our children unaccompanied at all, and there are occasional news stories of children being snatched from outside shops or even phone boxes, it is very difficult to understand what Jesus was up to in this story. As parents, we would be incredibly worried if our children went missing for three days (and so we should be). However, the situation was rather different in biblical times.

Maybe a fair comparison would be something that happened to us one Sunday. Jacqui had been out of the main part of the church when the children returned from their groups for Communion. When she returned, she saw that Natalie, our five-year-old daughter, was not sitting on the pew beside her brother. Immediately Jacqui began to worry. She started to search the building. She looked in the Junior Church rooms, the toilets, the street outside, but Natalie was not to be found. Eventually Jacqui looked in the book corner in the back of church, where Natalie always goes after the service, and sure enough she was sitting there with her head in a book. Natalie was in the most predictable place for her to be, just as Jesus was. Sometimes as parents, however, we are so busy running around that we cannot see what should be obvious about our children.

Jesus was not defying his parents by sitting with and listening to the teachers in the temple and questioning them. He was simply doing what was second nature to him. He wanted to spend time in his Father's house in order to learn. Children are naturally inquisitive and will often ask difficult questions in their search for knowledge, and we need as parents to feed that interest from a very early age. The level at which that communication happens will vary from child to child and at different ages, but even a fairly young baby will begin to coo and gurgle if they are spoken to. This is important for their speech development later on, and can be a very rewarding and special time as a new parent. We need to feed their inquisitive minds.

Towards the end of today's passage we read that Jesus was obedient to his parents (v. 51). If we want our children to grow up being obedient to us, it is up to us to teach them this obedience. We cannot rely on teachers, Sunday school teachers, nannies or child-minders to teach our children respect and obedience if we do not do it first, and require them to show respect for those in authority over them. As parents, we need to take responsibility for our children's actions and reactions to others. We need to shape them, so that they learn to obey those in authority over them, and respect other people. Other people can reinforce these principles, but it is a parental responsibility to teach them. Obedience does not come naturally to children; rather, they have to learn it.

There is another principle that we can learn from this reading from Luke 2. It is found in verse 51 where we read, 'His mother treasured all these things in her heart.' Throughout Luke's account of the early years of Jesus' life, references are made to how Mary dwelt on and marvelled at the things her son did and things said about him (for example, Luke 2:19).

When you first have a baby, everyone always tells you that they grow up quickly, and that you should record in some way the dates on which they start doing things—the first smile, the first time they roll over by themselves, the first word and so on. Shops are now full of 'Baby's first years' books with pages to fill in to record all the momentous events in your child's life. Although you may not feel the need to invest in a book, you will not regret writing things down. However long the first few weeks of a baby's life may seem to exhausted parents, our memories fade quickly, and later on we will appreciate looking back and remembering some of the precious moments that we had with our now-grown child.

One of our regrets is that we didn't write down things that our children said as toddlers. We can remember that Natalie referred to a close friend whose name is Penny as 'Ninny', but that is only because in some circles the name has stuck! But many of the phrases and words used by the children have been lost forever. At the time, we think we will never forget them because they were used so frequently or were so special, but once they are no longer a part of our everyday lives they are more difficult to remember. It doesn't take long to keep some kind of record of the classic statements and funny moments that our children give us as they grow up. We have recently invested in a photo album which gives spaces for comments alongside the photographs, and we are using this to try to record some of the special moments a bit more meticulously. Other people may find that the purchase of a video camera helps to store some memories.

The new lifestyle that we develop as a parent can at times seem so all-encompassing that we can not imagine a time when things will be different, and so we do not treasure the special moments. Then, all too soon, that phase in our child's life is over (although at the time it may not seem too soon to us!) and unless we have recorded these precious times we will forget them. So it is worth following Mary's example, and finding a way to treasure the milestones in your child's development.

**Prayer**

*Father God, we ask that you would help us to store away our memories of the special moments as our children grow up, so that when they are grown we would continue to find joy in those recollections. Help us also to respond to our children's curiosity and search for knowledge, and so allow them the space to learn and to grow. Amen*

# Love your children

**Titus 2:1–6 (NRSV)**

But as for you, teach what is consistent with sound doctrine. Tell the older men to be temperate, serious, prudent, and sound in faith, in love, and in endurance. Likewise, tell the older women to be reverent in behaviour, not to be slanderers or slaves to drink; they are to teach what is good, so that they may encourage the young women to love their husbands, to love their children, to be self-controlled, chaste, good managers of the household, kind, being submissive to their husbands, so that the word of God may not be discredited.

Likewise, urge the younger men to be self-controlled.

If we asked the question, 'What is the most important quality for successful parenting?' most people, Christian or not, would answer, 'Love for your children'. Whilst people may disagree fiercely about how children are to be brought up, it is generally agreed that they need to be brought up in an atmosphere of love. So we might expect the Bible to be full of commands to parents to love their children, and yet this is not the case. In fact, the requirement that older Christian women should encourage younger ones to love their children, which we find in today's reading, is the clearest such command. Otherwise there is a reference to slaves refusing their freedom because of love for their children in Exodus 21:5, a comment to the effect that loving parents discipline their children in Proverbs 13:24, and references in 4 Maccabees 14 and 15, in the Apocrypha, to a mother who allowed her seven sons to be killed rather than deny her faith. Why does the Bible not teach more clearly that we are to love our children? There are at least three possible reasons.

First of all, the Bible, and in particular the New Testament, seems to assume that people will love their children. We are taught to do the things which we might not be expected to do, not the things that people do almost instinctively. So in Matthew 5:43–46, for example,

Jesus teaches that his followers should not love their friends and hate their enemies as everyone else does, but should learn to love their enemies too. Love for friends is assumed, and it may be that love for children is assumed too. In fact, the Bible cautions us about our love for our children, that it shouldn't become idolatrous, but must be less than our love for God. We see that generally in the biblical teaching about love for God coming first (in Matthew 22, for example) and in the story of Abraham and Isaac (Genesis 22).

Secondly, the Bible often seems to be most concerned about how we actually live, rather than what we feel. This is certainly true in much of what the Bible has to say about love. For example, Jesus in his teaching about love in John's Gospel says, 'If you love me, you will keep my commandments' (John 14:15). Love, in other words, is demonstrated by what we do, not primarily by what we claim to feel. The story of Peter demonstrates the point. Peter was the disciple most given to declarations of love for Jesus. It was Peter who said to him, 'Though all become deserters because of you, I will never desert you', shortly before denying him (Matthew 26:33). When Jesus subsequently asked Peter to declare his love, he made it clear to him that love was to result in practical action. 'Do you love me? ... Feed my sheep' (John 21:17). So the Bible never tells us to love our children, but as we have seen elsewhere in this book it tells us to train them, to teach them the way of the Lord, not to exasperate them, to discipline them, and so on. Whilst the feelings we may associate with love are not commanded, the actions we associate with love most certainly are.

Thirdly, the Bible, and especially the Old Testament, does much of its teaching through stories, some of which we have already looked at. There are stories of people who sought children as a gift from God, for example Hannah in 1 Samuel 1. There are stories of parents who had to learn to put God ahead even of their children, for example Abraham in Genesis 22. There are stories of great heroes whose family lives were a disaster, notably David in 2 Samuel. There are stories of a mother's love towards her child, for example Mary's tenderness towards Jesus in the Gospels of Matthew and Luke. Some of these stories are put before us as examples to aspire to, and some as cautionary tales from which we should take warning.

It is clear, not least from our reading for today, that the Bible does teach by command and example that we should love our children. But more than that, it fills out for us the content of that love. In our society, love for children is held up as the golden rule of parenting, and yet there is little agreement about what that love should look like. How to discipline, what values to pass on, what kind of education to provide, how strict or permissive to be—these are all hotly contested issues amongst parents and child psychologists, most of whom would agree that love is the foundation of all good parenting. So the Bible goes further than merely telling us that we should love our children. It shows us how to do it.

**Prayer**

*Heavenly Father, we thank you that you love us as our own children, and that in your love you teach us, train us, and show us how to live. We pray that you would help us to love our children, when things are difficult as well as when things are easy, and that from your word you would teach us what that love should look like. We ask this through Jesus, your Son and our Lord. Amen*

# Favouritism

**Genesis 37:2–5 (NRSV)**

This is the story of the family of Jacob. Joseph, being seventeen years old, was shepherding the flock with his brothers; he was a helper to the sons of Bilhah and Zilpah, his father's wives; and Joseph brought a bad report of them to their father. Now Israel loved Joseph more than any other of his children, because he was the son of his old age; and he had made him a long robe with sleeves. But when his brothers saw that their father loved him more than all his brothers, they hated him, and could not speak peaceably to him.

Once Joseph had a dream, and when he told it to his brothers, they hated him even more.

In the previous reading, we saw how the Bible teaches us about love within families largely through stories, and today we have one such story as our reading. There is no doubt that Jacob loved Joseph deeply, and his generosity towards Joseph is evidence for this. But the Bible is painfully realistic about human experience, and in this story we see a parental love which is fundamentally flawed. Jacob loved Joseph more than any of his other children, and everyone knew it. So the effect of his love for his son was to stir up resentment and hatred within his family.

Today we would say that Jacob was guilty of favouritism. That is, he favoured Joseph over his other children and made no secret of it. Jacob lived in a culture which actually promoted favouritism, particularly, but not exclusively, towards male children over their female counterparts. Additionally, the firstborn son was generally regarded as being the most important child and the heir to all the family had, and we know from other Old Testament stories that parental favour given to one child and denied to another was not uncommon. For example, in Genesis 25:28 we read that Jacob himself was loved by his mother, while his father preferred his twin Esau. So there was nothing very surprising about the fact that Jacob showed favouritism to one of his sons.

Nowadays most people would regard favouritism towards one child as a bad thing, and yet many parents still struggle with it at times. Favouritism can take one of two main forms. Firstly, there may be a kind of emotional favouritism that only the parent involved may be aware of. That is to say, a parent actually experiences more loving feelings towards one child, even if he or she doesn't show it in action. Secondly, there is favouritism in behaviour, which may well be perceptible to other people, including the children involved. Jacob, of course, both felt and showed favouritism, but today parents who appear to favour one child may not be doing so out of a greater love for that child at all. It may be, for example, that one child is physically weaker or in poorer health, and parents develop a habit of being gentler with that child, which may continue even if health and strength improve. It may be that a child who was not expected to live, or who was born later in life, is treated differently. This doesn't necessarily happen consciously, but may simply become the norm.

But even if all of these factors are outside our experience, even if we are certain we love all our children equally, there are times when it is difficult to avoid the perception of favouritism. For example, many parents find that one child is going through a particularly delightful phase, just at the time when another is being especially horrible. While the four-year-old is learning to read and experimenting with words, or making exciting new friends and discoveries at school or nursery, the two-year-old may be pushing all the boundaries and being as difficult as possible. We may feel that we are always praising the older and shouting at the younger.

Many parents who love their children equally can end up appearing to show favouritism by overcompensating when a child does not live up to parental hopes and expectations. Perhaps one child is not as quick in reading or speaking as his elder sibling, and in order to build up his confidence parents constantly praise him for the steps forward that he does take. Meanwhile the older child sees a higher level of affirmation being given to reward less achievement, and can become resentful. Alternatively, a child who appears to be naughtier may be praised or rewarded for reaching a standard of behaviour that would be considered barely acceptable in a sibling. This can lead to a sense on the part of the other child that he or she is not loved as unconditionally.

The solution to favouritism is consistency in our love for our children. This means that our children know where they stand with us. They know that they are loved, accepted, affirmed. They know that we believe the best of them and want the best for them, that even when we correct or discipline them we are doing so out of love. This applies whether we have one child or many.

This is also the solution to the temptation to overcompensate. Encouragement and affirmation given to one child needs to be matched by praise expressed to the others. We don't have to do this in a very self-conscious way, so that whenever we pay a compliment to one child we immediately pay compliments to the others. But we do need to make sure that we are giving lots of encouragement and affirmation to each child overall. It is important to do something similar with time-allocation. One child may seem to need more attention than her siblings. But other children may feel they are not as important to us if we don't spend real, quality time with them too.

Consistent, healthy love requires effort and hard work. It is also strengthened by partnership. We can help our spouses by gently pointing out their blind spots, and talking together about our feelings towards our children. It can help to be able to express frustration with a child to a spouse or a friend, so that it doesn't explode in our relationship with the child. During periods when a child is giving particular heartache, it can be helpful to work out a strategy, together with our spouse, for dealing with them and our other children. Generally speaking, children grow out of these difficult phases. Our aim must be to ensure that they do so knowing that we love them, and our other children, consistently and equally.

**Prayer**

*Dear Father, thank you that you love all your children equally. Please help us to do the same, and to show consistent love, encouragement, and affirmation, so that our children grow up secure in the knowledge of our love, and yours. Amen*

# A mother's love

**Exodus 2:1–9 (NRSV)**

Now a man from the house of Levi went and married a Levite woman. The woman conceived and bore a son; and when she saw that he was a fine baby, she hid him three months. When she could hide him no longer she got a papyrus basket for him, and plastered it with bitumen and pitch; she put the child in it and placed it among the reeds on the bank of the river. His sister stood at a distance, to see what would happen to him.

The daughter of Pharaoh came down to bathe at the river, while her attendants walked beside the river. She saw the basket among the reeds and sent her maid to bring it. When she opened it, she saw the child. He was crying, and she took pity on him. 'This must be one of the Hebrews' children,' she said. Then his sister said to Pharaoh's daughter, 'Shall I go and get you a nurse from the Hebrew women to nurse the child for you?' Pharaoh's daughter said to her, 'Yes.' So the girl went and called the child's mother. Pharaoh's daughter said to her, 'Take this child and nurse it for me, and I will give you your wages.' So the woman took the child and nursed it.

One of the striking things about biblical stories of relationships and family life is how they have the endless capacity to surprise and involve us. These are not sentimental fairy tales, promising happy endings for all, but complex stories of men and women alive in a tough world, making terrifying choices for the sake of their God and his people.

We see this in the bittersweet story of the first days of Moses. Born into a political culture of horrifying barbarity, he is destined for death before he has even had a chance to register the world around him. Yet the resourcefulness of his mother and sister bought him a future where other baby boys born at the same time had none.

Modern-day readers in the prosperous West may find the setting of this story so removed from their own experience that it is difficult to learn from it. Yet we don't have to look too far to find people whose family lives have faced them with similar cruel choices.

As we write, television news bulletins are full of images of Kosovan refugees, fleeing the nightmare of ethnic cleansing. Many have been separated from loved ones on their journey to safety. One man had lost his young daughter in the rush to leave, and had scoured refugee camps for her. Finally he had tracked her down, only to be told that he did not have the right paperwork to take her with him. He was given two minutes with his little girl before being escorted away. All he could do for her was to offer money to another family to care for her. In a world like this, a world like that of the Hebrews in Egypt, the rules of modern parenting take second place to more fundamental issues of survival.

And yet even for those of us whose lives seem comfortable and secure, there are things we can learn from this unnamed heroine of the Old Testament, some of which may serve as a corrective to a contemporary over-sentimental picture of parental love.

First of all, we see the tenderness of Moses' mother towards him. We picture her making the basket into which she is shortly to place her son, perhaps testing it in water to make sure it floats, perhaps crying while she works as she thinks of the moment she dreads when she will have to entrust her baby to the river and to God. Adversity had not made her harsh. Something about this baby had made her determined to save him. When she had seen him, she had recognized that he was 'a fine baby' (v. 2). This little boy had produced a feeling and then an action in her that was potentially dangerous, certainly foolish, and yet because of her tenderness towards him she could not resist.

Secondly, we see her resourcefulness, and that of her daughter. The absence of men-folk in this story does make one wonder where they were. Had they disassociated themselves from this madcap scheme? Did they simply lack the imagination to contribute? Either way, it is the women who exhibit the courage and quick thinking which make the plan work. In particular, the intervention of Moses' sister in having Pharaoh's daughter hire her mother as a wet-nurse is a brilliant move.

Thirdly, we see the commitment of these two women, even in the face of potential danger to themselves and the rest of their family. They were breaking the law, in a country which did not value Hebrew life at all. The consequences of being caught could have been severe, and the chances of it were high. One cry from the baby when the wrong person was nearby could have brought disaster, and all parents know how difficult it is to stop a baby crying, however desperately we might want to!

Fourthly, we see the practicality of the love of Moses' mother for him. This was not a sentimental love. In her heart of hearts, she must have known that there was not going to be any unambiguous happy ending to this story. Either the plan would fail and the whole family might be punished, or the plan would succeed and she would have to entrust her baby to a stranger for life. She can't have known that she would be asked to nurse her child. Even then, we don't know how much contact she had with her child after her nursing job was over. Despite all this, her love was hard-edged enough to do what was best for the child, however heartrending it was for her. Perhaps this hard-edged love is seen more commonly in situations like Kosovo, places of war or national disaster, where conditions are brutal in a way few of us can imagine.

Fortunately we don't face the terrifying choices that Moses' mother faced. But we can learn from her about having a love which is not soft or sentimental, but which is tough, courageous, resourceful, tender. The actions she took paved the way for Moses to grow into a man of huge significance for her people and the purposes of God. As we love our children with the same kind of love, we also will enable our children to grow to their full potential and to play their part in the world.

**Prayer**

*Heavenly Father, thank you that you regard every child as important and significant. Teach us as parents how to love our child with realistic and courageous love. May we learn from the example of Moses' mother how to do what is best for our child. Amen*

# Love always protects

**Matthew 2:13–15, 19–23 (NRSV)**

Now after they had left, an angel of the Lord appeared to Joseph in a dream and said, 'Get up, take the child and his mother, and flee to Egypt, and remain there until I tell you; for Herod is about to search for the child, to destroy him.' Then Joseph got up, took the child and his mother by night, and went to Egypt, and remained there until the death of Herod. This was to fulfil what had been spoken by the Lord through the prophet, 'Out of Egypt I have called my son.' ...

When Herod died, an angel of the Lord suddenly appeared in a dream to Joseph in Egypt and said, 'Get up, take the child and his mother, and go to the land of Israel, for those who were seeking the child's life are dead.' Then Joseph got up, took the child and his mother, and went to the land of Israel. But when he heard that Archelaus was ruling over Judea in place of his father Herod, he was afraid to go there. And after being warned in a dream, he went away to the district of Galilee. There he made his home in a town called Nazareth, so that what had been spoken through the prophets might be fulfilled, 'He will be called a Nazorean.'

At the time of writing, we are preparing to move. We will have a new house (well, new to us), a new church, new neighbours. The children will go to a new school, and make new friends. Although we will remain in the same city, London, the distance is such that we might as well be moving to another part of the country altogether.

Moving can be traumatic for children. They grow up in one place, and assume they will be there for ever. In times gone by, of course, they probably would have been. But in our increasingly mobile society, many children will face the challenge of settling somewhere new at least once in their childhood.

In Matthew 2 we read about a move that Jesus and his family were compelled to make when he was very young. This was not a planned move. It was not a step along the road to a better job or a nicer area. It was an urgent move, under the cover of darkness, to escape a real and potent danger. It was also a move to a different country, a different culture, not just to the other side of the city as ours is going to be. For a Hebrew family, there would be great irony in fleeing to Egypt. Egypt, after all, was the place from which the Israelites had fled to the security of the promised land. Now the promised land had become too dangerous for God's Son, and, for that matter, for other boys of his age whose parents were not warned to escape, and who suffered the consequences of Herod's evil rage.

In this story we see one of the strongest of parental emotions, the desire to protect your child. Joseph and Mary left friends, family, the temple and synagogue, their country, in order to protect Jesus. In the same way that we have seen Moses' mother taking practical, costly steps to save the life of her son, so Joseph and Mary sacrificed almost everything to secure Jesus' safety. Once again the parallels and contrasts between the two stories are striking. In both instances we see that when a child is in danger, a loving parent will do whatever it takes to protect him or her.

All of us who are parents feel that protective instinct in different ways, and it is right that we should. In our family at the moment, we are trying hard to protect our children from the negative consequences of our impending move. We tell them interesting stories and facts about our new neighbourhood, whilst trying not to discuss the move in their hearing too much. We are trying to ensure that they transfer to a school which is as good as the one they are currently in. We are praying for their sense of security during a time of change. In other families the protective instinct will be seen in different ways, but it will generally be present.

But there is a danger here as well, that as parents we become over-protective. When we are being over-protective we deny our children the opportunity to grow up, to become the people they will be. We also deny that God, who is with our children even when we are not, is to be trusted in caring for them. An over-protective parent forgets that pain is a vital part of maturing, and tries to prevent it in every situation. So, for example, when a child comes home complaining that their homework is too difficult, an over-protective parent will immediately ask the teacher to make it easier. Or when a child has been upset by a friend, an over-protective parent will suggest that they break the friendship rather than work through the problem.

As parents, we walk a tightrope as we seek to be protective of our children's well-being without mollycoddling them. We need to keep re-evaluating how we do this, particularly as our children grow older. Throughout, our goal must be to assure our children of our love and support, offering protection from real danger but also allowing them to explore and to grow. Even for Mary, there were times when she had to face the fact that her son was growing up and his relationship with her had changed (for examples, see Luke 2:48–49, and Matthew 12:46–50).

Jesus was partially shaped by all these experiences, and identified by them. Other people were not always sure where he was from. Our readings today identify him as someone who had come 'out of Egypt' and also from Nazareth in Galilee. At a time when being from somewhere was important, Jesus seemed to have come from nowhere and everywhere. As someone who moved around a great deal as a child, Stephen can identify with this. There is a feeling of rootlessness which comes when the answer to the polite question 'Where are you from?' takes five minutes to give. But God took that rootlessness in Jesus' background and used it as Jesus became the One who could save men and women and children from every place.

**Prayer**

*Thank you, Father God, for the protective love that you give us for our child. Thank you that you too have a protective love for us, your children. Please help us to know how to protect without becoming over-protective, so that our child can grow to reach his or her full potential. Amen*

# I love you, but...

**John 15:9–17 (NRSV)**

'As the Father has loved me, so I have loved you; abide in my love. If you keep my commandments, you will abide in my love, just as I have kept my Father's commandments and abide in his love. I have said these things to you so that my joy may be in you, and that your joy may be complete.

'This is my commandment, that you love one another as I have loved you. No one has greater love than this, to lay down one's life for one's friends. You are my friends if you do what I command you. I do not call you servants any longer, because the servant does not know what the master is doing; but I have called you friends, because I have made known to you everything that I have heard from my Father. You did not choose me but I chose you. And I appointed you to go and bear fruit, fruit that will last, so that the Father will give you whatever you ask him in my name. I am giving you these commands so that you may love one another.'

Jacqui remembers that when she worked with people with severe learning difficulties, one thing that she occasionally found herself saying was, 'I like you, but I do not always like the way you behave!' It is possible and completely normal to like people, even love them, but not always appreciate the particular behaviour that they are displaying. Love sometimes comes completely naturally to us—towards particular people at particular times it flows quite effortlessly from us—but at other times, even for those same people, it can be a real effort.

In the passage that we read today from John, Jesus commands his followers to love one another. A part of keeping Christ's commandments to us is to love one another. But this is not a sentimental 'warm and fuzzy' feeling that can be swayed by an action or deed. It is a deep-rooted, gritty love which is prepared to risk any type of personal sacrifice, even the loss of one's own life if that is the best thing for, or would save, the person who is loved. To achieve that type of love, we need to work on loving those around us.

Some people find it very easy to love a newborn baby. Others find that it takes them more time before they can look at the child in their arms and say from deep within their heart, 'I love you'. Whichever is true for you, at times in the future your love for your child is likely to be more of a struggle. You may find yourself thinking or even saying, 'I love you, but I do not always love the way you behave!'

When we look down at our new baby, we will often feel overwhelmed with feelings of love for them. For some reason the top of a newborn baby's head is unbelievably kissable! Then sometimes we look at them when they have been crying for what seems like hours and nothing that we do seems to calm them down, and it is then difficult to feel anything but frustration towards them. At that moment, love can seem like more of an effort.

As our relationship with our child develops and changes over time, there will be phases when it will be very easy to love them. The happy baby who lies cooing and giggling on a mat, responding with a smile to anyone who takes a moment to say 'hello', is enough to melt the toughest heart. However, there will also be times when it is more of a struggle, when obeying Jesus' command to love as he loved takes a decision of the will, when it feels that we have nothing left to give to the small, screaming child who will not be pacified. At times like this, we need to abide in the love of Jesus, and this alone will give us the resources to go on showing love for our child.

During the first few months after a baby is born into a family, our physical resources as parents are often depleted, due to lack of sleep, new demands and, particularly as a mother, breast-feeding. (No one ever tells you how physically draining that is until you stop and realize that you did not always feel quite so bad!) We have said before that it is when we are tired that our true personality shows through, and this is also true for our partners. The stress of a new child can lead our husband or wife to behave in ways which we find difficult to tolerate, and this means that sometimes we will have to work hard at our love for them as well. If our love is a deep-rooted one, not based on volatile feelings but on commitment and mutual support, then it will be much easier for us to weather these more testing stages of our relationship.

When Jesus commanded his disciples to love one another he knew that at times it would be hard. Loving another person consistently is hard at times because, in our humanity, all of us occasionally disappoint ourselves as well as those who love us. We will not always live up to our own or our spouse's expectations and therefore at times we are bound to hurt those whom we love and who love us. If in our love we are striving for what is best for the other person, it will sometimes mean not having or doing what we personally want most but seeking to bring fulfilment to the one we love. This is true for our children and our wife or husband. Only as we spend time with Jesus, meditating on and experiencing his love, will we be able to start offering others love like that.

**Prayer**

*Heavenly Father, thank you that you love us. Teach us how to love with the unselfish love with which Christ loved his disciples. May our love for each other and our child be deep-rooted, so that it can withstand any difficult stages in our lives together. Amen*

# Putting God first

**Genesis 22:1–18 (NRSV)**

After these things God tested Abraham. He said to him, 'Abraham!' And he said, 'Here I am.' He said, 'Take your son, your only son Isaac, whom you love, and go to the land of Moriah, and offer him there as a burnt offering on one of the mountains that I shall show you.' So Abraham rose early in the morning, saddled his donkey, and took two of his young men with him, and his son Isaac; he cut the wood for the burnt offering, and set out and went to the place in the distance that God had shown him. On the third day Abraham looked up and saw the place far away. Then Abraham said to his young men, 'Stay here with the donkey; the boy and I will go over there; we will worship, and then we will come back to you.' Abraham took the wood of the burnt offering and laid it on his son Isaac, and he himself carried the fire and the knife. So the two of them walked on together. Isaac said to his father Abraham, 'Father!' And he said, 'Here I am, my son.' He said, 'The fire and the wood are here, but where is the lamb for a burnt offering?' Abraham said, 'God himself will provide the lamb for a burnt offering, my son.' So the two of them walked on together.

When they came to the place that God had shown him, Abraham built an altar there and laid the wood in order. He bound his son Isaac, and laid him on the altar, on top of the wood. Then Abraham reached out his hand and took the knife to kill his son. But the angel of the Lord called to him from heaven, and said, 'Abraham, Abraham!' And he said, 'Here I am.' He said, 'Do not lay your hand on the boy or do anything to him; for now I know that you fear God, since you have not withheld your son, your only son, from me.' And Abraham looked up and saw a ram, caught in a thicket by its horns. Abraham went and took the ram and offered it up as a burnt offering instead of his son. So Abraham called that place 'The Lord will provide'; as it is said to this day, 'On the mount of the Lord it shall be provided.' The angel of the Lord called to Abraham a second time from heaven, and said, 'By myself I have sworn, says the Lord: Because you have done this, and have not withheld your son, your only son, I will indeed bless you, and I will make your offspring as numerous as the stars of heaven and as the sand that is on the seashore. And your offspring shall possess the gate of their enemies, and by your offspring shall all the nations of the earth gain blessing for themselves, because you have obeyed my voice.'

The Bible teaches that God requires our first loyalty. We may have many other wonderful things in our lives—family, friends, a successful career. But everything else is to take second place to God. The Old Testament law and prophets insist on it. Jesus reaffirms it, when he tells us that by comparison with our love for him our love for even our family should look like hatred (Luke 14:26).

The story of Abraham and his willingness to sacrifice his son Isaac makes the same point in narrative form. The idea that God might require someone literally to sacrifice his children is found only here in scripture, and stands out all the more starkly as a result. In fact, one of the things that marked out the people of Israel from some of their neighbouring communities in the ancient world was their abhorrence of human sacrifice, something which God never required from them. But in this incident God challenges Abraham in order to find out to whom Abraham had given his first loyalty. Abraham loved Isaac, but he loved God more.

Abraham didn't actually have to make such a momentous sacrifice, his willingness was enough. But occasionally Christians have faced such a choice. A story is told of a Christian minister in a time and place where brutal persecution of the Church was the norm. On one occasion he was arrested and threatened with execution. He was prepared for this. Other Christians had faced martyrdom courageously, and he was ready to accept it too. Seeing that he was unbowed, his tormentors had his wife and children arrested as well, and told him that unless he denied his faith his family would die with him. Now he was afraid and confused. How could he sacrifice his children for his faith? He was about to agree to his captor's demands when his wife spoke to him. 'Remember what Jesus did for us. We can't deny him now.' The minister affirmed his faith in Christ, and he and his family paid the price.

God doesn't require this kind of sacrifice from many of us, but he does sometimes require sacrifice of a more everyday kind, or at least the willingness to make such a sacrifice. These sacrifices may affect our children as well as us. They might include going without a family holiday in order to give a sum of money away, or sacrificing a degree of privacy in order to open our home to a guest for a while.

We mentioned earlier that at the time of writing we are preparing to move to a new church in another part of our city. As it became known that we were looking for a new appointment, we were approached by a number of people and asked to consider applying for jobs which they were looking to fill. Almost as soon as we had been approached about a particular vacancy, we would get out our copy of the Schools League Tables, and start looking up Ofsted reports on the Internet, trying to discover what the local schools were like. While we were prepared to move to a tough area, or to accept a challenging job, we wanted to make sure that our children would not have to sacrifice their chance of a reasonable education. Yet still there was a niggling question in the back of our minds. What if God calls us to a place where the schools are bad? Might he not want us to sacrifice our children's schooling in order to serve him?

Of course it is right that we should seek to protect our children. We looked recently at the protective nature of parental love, and saw that this is an important part of our responsibility for our children. Yet even when we feel we are doing the best for our children, it is all too easy for us to sacrifice them in unconscious ways. Some parents are so concerned about being successful in their careers that they have little time for their children. If they aren't at work, they are tired and irritable from the stresses of a long day. Others sacrifice their children to the local church. They are at so many meetings, so busy with Christian activities, that they never seem to have time for their family responsibilities. Of course it is good to be actively involved in the local church. But if we have to step down from the church council or from leading a housegroup for a while, someone else can usually be found to undertake that task. If we don't have the time to be with and care for our children properly, nobody else will step in and do that for us. These are sacrifices that by and large God does not require of us.

God does still ask us to give him our first loyalty. There may be difficult times in our lives when we have to demonstrate that we have done so. But for the most part, God wants us to express our love for him, at least in part, by the tender, passionate, whole-hearted way we reveal his love to those he has placed around us, including our children.

**Prayer**

*Father God, you were prepared to sacrifice your Son Jesus Christ, because of your great love for us and for all your creation. Please help us to love you most of all, so that our lives might reflect the priorities of your Kingdom. Amen*

# Children of God

### 1 John 3:1–2 (NRSV)

See what love the Father has given us, that we should be called children of God; and that is what we are. The reason the world does not know us is that it did not know him. Beloved, we are God's children now; what we will be has not yet been revealed. What we do know is this: when he is revealed, we will be like him, for we will see him as he is.

Our final reading in this book reminds us of the 'big picture' in which we care for and raise our children. It talks to us about God's love for us, about our identity as his children, and about our hope for the future. Four points in particular stand out.

First of all, we are reminded that love comes from God. 'See what love the Father has given us,' John writes in verse 1. All true love comes from God. It is his invention and his gift, and wherever we experience love as God designed it we experience a touch of his love. The important thing for us as new parents is that our relationship with God is based on his love for us first and foremost, not our love for him, which is a weak thing by comparison. This is important to us now because often the first few months of a child's life are the hardest in which to love and serve God as we may have done in the past. We feel too tired to pray or study the Bible very much. We can't be as involved in church activities as we were before. We may feel irritable and distinctly unspiritual. When we feel like this, we need to remember that it is God who holds on to us by his love, not we who hold on to him by what we do for him.

Secondly, we learn from this passage that we are God's children. Verse 1 says, 'We [are] called children of God; and that is what we are.' This means, of course, that our son or daughter is also a child of God, and should be treated with all the love and tenderness and respect that a child of God deserves. It also means that if we are looking for a model for parenting, we can look at how God deals with us. This is significant in a society where many people have unhappy memories of their own upbringing. If we don't feel that our parents made a good job of raising us, how do we learn how to care for our children? The answer may lie in looking at God's nurture of us. We see in his relationship with his children tender love and longing, sacrifice and compassion, anger and mercy. From meditating on what the Bible shows of his love and character, particularly in the person of Jesus, we can learn how to show the same love to our children.

Thirdly, we remember as we read this passage that we look forward as Christians to a future which is unknown but full of hope and expectation. We will see Christ in his glory, and will be made like him. We live in a world where people generally think about the future with great pessimism. They expect economic slowdown, war and oppression, escalating crime, and declining standards of living. Christians don't necessarily think that none of these things will happen, but we have hope in the midst of life for the coming of God's Kingdom. Similarly, we don't know what the future holds for our child or for our family life, and yet as parents we look forward with hope and expectation. We know that each new phase in our child's life is full of possibilities and challenges, and that ultimately we are in God's hands, so we can contemplate the future confidently.

Finally, John teaches us that we who know and love God are becoming more like him. 'What we do know is this: when he is revealed, we will be like him, for we will see him as he is' (v. 2). This will happen completely when Christ returns and all darkness and evil in the world and in us are finally swept away, but it is also happening now, as we experience the love of the Father in our own lives. As we open our lives to God's love, we are increasingly able to show love to others, not least to our children. And that love is at the heart of good parenting. We can learn skills and techniques, read books and attend courses, but without love we will not be good parents. With love, we may make mistakes and fail our children in many ways, but they will grow up secure, knowing that they are accepted and cherished just for being themselves. This is the love that comes from God, and we can pass it on only as we open our lives to experience it ourselves.

So in the end, good parenting comes down to the basics of the gospel—that God loves us, he has shown his love for us in Jesus and that through Jesus we can know his love and his transforming power in our lives day by day, and his grace and forgiveness when we get it wrong. That gospel is the foundation of all successful living, and the best start we can give to our children is to live it and teach it so that it becomes the basis for their lives as children and later on as adults too.

**Prayer**

*Father God, thank you that by your love and power you are making us more like you. Please help us as parents to reflect your gospel in all that we say and do, so that it might shape our children and become the foundation of their lives. Amen*

*New Daylight* is ideal for those looking for a fresh, devotional approach to reading and understanding the Bible. Each issue covers four months of daily Bible reading and reflection with each day offering a Bible passage (text included), helpful comment and a prayer or thought for the day ahead.

The notes are edited by David Winter, an Anglican priest in the Diocese of Oxford, former BBC Head of Religious Broadcasting at the BBC, and regular contributor to Thought for the Day and Prayer for Today. *New Daylight* is written by a gifted team of contributors including Adrian Plass, Brother Ramon, Hilary McDowell, Marcus Maxwell, Margaret Cundiff, Henry Wansbrough, Rosemary Green, Rob Gillion, Graham Dodds and Peter Graves.

*New Daylight* is also available in large print and on cassette for the visually impaired.

## NEW DAYLIGHT SUBSCRIPTIONS

❑ I would like to give a gift subscription
(please complete both name and address sections below)

❑ I would like to take out a subscription myself
(complete name and address details only once)

This completed coupon should be sent with appropriate payment to BRF. Alternatively, please write to us quoting your name, address, the subscription you would like for either yourself or a friend (with their name and address), the start date and credit card number, expiry date and signature if paying by credit card.

Gift subscription name ______________________

Gift subscription address ______________________

______________________ Postcode ____________

**Please send to the above, beginning with the May 2000 issue:**

| (please tick box) | UK | SURFACE | AIR MAIL |
|---|---|---|---|
| NEW DAYLIGHT | ❑ £10.20 | ❑ £11.55 | ❑ £13.50 |
| NEW DAYLIGHT 3-year sub | ❑ £25.00 | | |

Please complete the payment details below and send your coupon, with appropriate payment to: **The Bible Reading Fellowship, Peter's Way, Sandy Lane West, Oxford OX4 5HG**

Your name ______________________

Your address ______________________

______________________ Postcode ____________

Total enclosed £ __________ (cheques should be made payable to 'BRF')

Payment by cheque ❑ postal order ❑ Visa ❑ Mastercard ❑ Switch ❑

Card number: ❑❑❑❑ ❑❑❑❑ ❑❑❑❑ ❑❑❑❑

Expiry date of card: ❑❑❑❑ Issue number (Switch): ❑❑❑❑

Signature (essential if paying by credit/Switch card) ______________________

NB: BRF notes are also available from your local Christian bookshop. **BRF is a Registered Charity**

E26